POLITICS IN INDIA

GE - 2: FOR B.A. 2ND SEMESTER
STUDENTS OF BODOLAND UNIVERSITY

RITURAJ BASUMATARY

Contents

Approaches to study the Nature of Indian state and Politics

Approaches to study the Nature of Indian state and Politics

'State' is the most commonly used term in politics. Up to the first half of twentieth century, political science was concerned with the study of the phenomenon of the state in its varied aspects and relationship, as distinct from family, tribe, and nation and from all private associations and groups. As Garner put it, political science begins and ends with the state'. Gettle, Gilchrist etc. have also been the representatives of such a school of political thought. Etymologically, a state is organized machinery for the making and carrying out of political decisions and for the enforcement of the laws and rules of a government. According to Garner, 'the state, as a concept of political science and public law is a community of persons more or less numerous, permanently occupying a definite portion of territory control and possessing an organized government to which the great body, of inhabitants render habitual obedience. According to this definition, population, fixed territory, government and sovereignty are the essential elements of the state. Different from society, government, association and the nations, the state is considered a distinct institution. The state is a central player in the modern drama of development, and nowhere is it more important than in the development of the third world. Its successes, its failures and its distortions cannot be fully appreciated without a proper understanding of the trajectories of state formation. To understand how states are forward and how they have come to be what they are, we must think historically, about them, and look beyond the formal structures to their social and political specifications. Modern state may be classified into two broad forms-liberal democratic and totalitarian. While the former stands on the foundation of democracy signifying residence of power in the hands of the people and its utilization by their chosen representatives; the latter is antithetic of the former where political power is in the hands of a group of power hungry politician or a junta of military oligarchs who strive to severe legitimacy of their rule by means of force and fraud'. Another variety popularly known by the name of 'welfare state' has emerged. The concept welfare state has been devised to meet the challenge of the totalitarian state. Various attempts have been made to understand the politics of India. Though there is no rational view on the formation of the state but mainly two approaches interpret the nature of the Indian states. These are liberal and Marxist.

Liberal Approach

The liberal approach stressed on institution and processes as the key to understanding the state and political power. It recognises the need for development and social change. To study the nature of any particular state, it is necessary to analyse the relation between state, power, and social classes and the purpose of the state. The liberal democratic form stands on 7 the foundation of democracy. It sees the state as a democratic state where rule of the people is implemented with freedom of speech and expression, free and periodic elections, a responsible and accountable government, independent judiciary, rule of law etc. Through rule of law it prevents chaos and anarchy in the society which restricts absolute freedom but creates freedom within the law for all citizens. This approach emphasised the primacy and independence of political processes. This is evident from the writings of Rajni Kothari, S. Rudolph and F. Frankel. Liberal scholars have stressed the need of acceptance of the centrality of state as an autonomous actors or relative autonomy, where state has to play a highly Interventionist developmental role. Further rule of one party in India i.e. Congress party's dominance for nearly four decades had helped to strengthen the political base for the emergence of a strong state. It emerged as Independent from colonial rule under Indian national Congress which transformed itself into a ruling party and acquired the characteristic of an accommodating party. Political scientists like Rajni Kothari, Norman Palmer and Morris Jones have subscribed to the Liberal modernist perspective. Rajni Kothari commented on Indian model as a society of 'dominant political centre' which is characterised by plural identities. He considered the existence of pluralist tolerance and a genius for integration as the important factors for the successful establishment of Democracy in India. Morris Jones focus was on the working of political institutions and processes to understand the nature of state in India. He gave the importance to Democratic institutions in bringing the transformation at different levels. He stressed on the "capability of political institutions in bringing about economic and social change". It was assumed that "with a liberal democratic constitutional system and universal suffrage, the Indian political system would gradually develop its own processes of democratic decision-making, rational administration, and modern citizenship". This combination of "democratic ideology, economic development, distributive justice provided a unique opportunity of transforming a traditionally apolitical society in which the state became the central instrument and politics the principal agent of transformation. This shows the optimistic picture of political institutions and democratic processes. The liberal critique of the Indian state can be read in the writings of Rajni Kothari, Atul Kohli, The Rudolphs, Gunnar Myrdal. Gunnar Myrdal criticized the inability of the state to enforce public policies to eradicate poverty or to enforce laws and dubbed the institutional model of the Indian state as "soft state". According to Myrdal, the Indian state was soft as it had no power to rectify institutions that stood in the way of reform and development. As a result, it could not tackle the institution of caste directly, take measures of effective land reform, eradicate corruption or enforce ideas of development effectively through the people. One consequence of this softness has been the growth of left-wing extremism, which Manmohan Singh called the "gravest internal threat" to the country's security. Myrdal's 'hard state ' would have been able to tackle Naxalism which has gravely affected the nation. The liberal approach focuses on institutions and processes to understand state and political power in India. The state is considered the central instrument of social progress and principal agent of transformation. According to the Rudolphs, there are two groups characterised in the Indian state, one being the 'owners of production' and the other being the 'labourer' group. They analysed the state as a mediator between these two conflicting groups, and in doing so, must remain autonomous in order to maintain structural unity of the state. The role of the state would hence be the "third actor". The Rudolphs believe in the Indian state as a weak – strong state. It is strong because of large basic industries, ideology of secularism Democracy, Socialism and mixed economy that has minimized conflicts. It is weak because of caste class conflicts, religious fundamentalism and communalism, rising levels of political mobilization etc.

Marxist Approach

Then there is Marxist approach where political economy is the vital factor. State is the most important vehicle of economic development. It ascribes a partisan role to the state in the ongoing class struggle between the ruling class and the ruled. Marxist would have described the Indian state responsible for constituting a social order which maintains hegemony of capital over labour and seeks to reproduce this relationship. This was the main intellectual counterpoint of western political thought, beginning with Plato and Aristotle. This considered the state essential to the maintenance of order and civilisation. Marxist argued that the state emerged historically along with the division of society into a ruling class that enjoyed leisure and privilege, while the mass of people were limited to make a living and were exploited as slaves and proletarians in the overall evolution of society from the ancient period to the modern one. Later Marx was convinced that the state could be abolished when the proletariat had won the class struggle, something that he believed was inevitable. Communist party of India describes India as a national bourgeoisie state which has the possibility of moving peacefully towards socialism by following a non-capitalist path of development. The Indian capitalist class is today, after more than five decades of post independence, a class which has expanded and undergone some important changes. At the time of independence itself, there was a big bourgeoisie, which dominated this class as a whole. But the outlook of this big bourgeoisie has undergone a significant change. It was the big bourgeoisie which spelt out the type of capitalist development that was undertaken in India from the 1950s: (a) a class which understood the international situation and its own base in Indian society. It needed the Indian State to accumulate capital and develop capitalism. The State capitalism, which the Indian ruling classes sponsored, played a two-fold role. It enabled the development of capitalism within a constrained framework. A model of capitalist development without a thoroughgoing agrarian revolution, which necessitated a compromise with landlordism and the development of agrarian capitalism from above relying on landlords and the rich peasants. (b) The subordinate position of the Indian bourgeoisie vis a vis world capitalism required the organic link with foreign finance capital and reliance on this imperialist capital to advance the path of capitalist development. (c) Such a capitalist development could have a relative degree of autonomy in a situation where there was the existence of the Soviet Union and a socialist bloc; the bourgeois-landlord classes in India could utilise the conflicts between the two blocs and manoeuvre to strengthen its own position to a limited extent. Academic Marxist like A.R. Desai called India a capitalist state. A "bourgeoisie constitution" as he named the Indian constitution, argued that initially inclusion of right to property in the constitution was to give the right to income through ownership which resulted in social inequalities. Further Indian Planning based on mixed economy accepted a class structure based on private ownership as the basis for economic development. He said the tilt of mixed economy is towards private sector. On the same lines, C.P. Bhambari has highlighted the conflict within the ruling classes and a relative weakening of the state. Hamza Alvi has argued that India as a post-colonial state had relative economy in mediating the competing interests of the ruling classes. There exist some specific conditions which helped the state to play an autonomous role in post-colonial states. He contends that there is no classbased politics in India and there are multi-class parties like Congress, the weakness of indigenous propertied class allows the Indian state a great measure of relative autonomy. On the same lines another scholar Partha Chatterjee says that there has been a coalition of dominant classes since independence. The power was shared with landed elites to exercise control over the state. A Marxist understanding of the Indian state shows the class character of the state, serving the dominant classes and using coercive means to safeguard their socio-economic structure, if need be.

Gandhian Approach

Gandhian approach to study the nature of state is based on the concept of Swaraj. It means absence of alien rule and establishment of self- Government. He considered state a necessary evil and supported Thoreau's dictum that "that Government is the best which governs the least". It says that Government is best when interference with people's liberties and rights is minimum. In Gandhi's assessment, the state (Western type) was the symbol of violence in concentrated form. In order to ensure allegiance from the citizens the state (which means its authority) applies coercion or violent measures mercilessly. Once he said, "the individual has a soul but the state is a soulless machine, the state can never be weaned away from violence to which it owes its existence". In other words, Gandhi treated both state and violence or coercion synonymous. He further says that there is a state but not violence or coercion in any form cannot be imagined. He gathered experience in South Africa that more and more power to the state meant more and more violence or greater amount of coercion. In the name of the maintenance of law and order the South Africa's white government acquired enormous power and this led to the ruthless administration, exploitation and curtailment of individuals' liberty. He once said that a political organisation based on violence would never receive his approval. Rather, he is always afraid of such an organisation. What he felt about the Western state system is quite explicit in a comment which he made, "I look upon an increase in the power of the state with greatest fear, because although while apparently doing good by minimising exploitation, it does the greatest harm to mankind by destroying individuality which is at the root of progress". From the above analysis it is absolutely clear that Gandhi rejected the state of Western model on the ground that it represented violence or coercion. Now the question is why did he oppose violence so much? The modern state, according to Gandhi, was about to destroy individuality—that individual freedom and spontaneous urge to work. Secondly, the individualism is the root cause of progress. Gandhi believed that nothing could be done by applying coercion. Again, the individual cannot be forced to do any work against his will or spontaneous desire. To put it in other words, according to Gandhi the progress of the society can be achieved through the functions which the individuals perform willingly. But Gandhi appears to us as more aggressive. Under any circumstances the individual's freedom cannot be sacrificed. Gandhi's love for individual's freedom ranks him with the great anarchist philosophers the central idea is that to Gandhi state is an undesirable political organisation because of its close connection with violence. Gandhi's Swaraj means Government by the consent and participation of the people. For him direct democracy is impossible in a large country like India. After independence the constitution makers of India adopted some features of Gandhian state. Some of these are stress on egalitarian Society, untouchability and special care towards the weaker sections of society. In fact, the wanted to establish decentralization of power through Panchayat Raj System all over India. Further he justified the existence of state in terms of the functions it performs, so long as and to the extent it performs the functions which lead to the good, welfare and upliftment of all human beings.

CHAPTER II

Indian Constitution: Basic Features, Debates on Fundamental Rights and Directive Principles

Basic Features of Indian Constitution

Indian Constitution was drafted in the mid-twentieth century. The Constitution makers drew inspiration from various sources and adopted various unique features to be incorporated in the Indian Constitution. Following are the salient features of Indian Constitution—

1. The largest Constitution : Sir Ivor Jennings has termed the Constitution of India as a largest and detailed Constitution of the world. Constitution originally consisted of 22 Parts, 395 Articles and 8 Schedules (Presently 12 Schedules).

2. Sovereign, Socialist, Secular, Democratic Republic : The source of Constitution is the people of India. According to Preamble the people of India have adopted, enacted and given to themselves the Constitution. It declares India to be Sovereign, Socialist, Secular and Democratic Republic. Words 'Socialist' and 'Secular' were added in Preamble by 42nd Constitutional Amendment, 1976.

3. Parliamentary form of Government : India has Parliamentary form of government both at the Centre and the States. In this form of government the President is the Constitutional Head of the State but the real executive power vests in Council of Ministers. They are responsible to the Legislature. India has followed British

model in this respect.

4. Fundamental Rights : The Fundamental Rights have been incorporated in Part Ill of the Constitution. These rights are against the State. State cannot make any law which violates the Fundamental Rights. Such laws are declared unconstitutional by the Supreme Court or High Court. Apart from these rights there is a strong provision for enforcement of these rights. Supreme Court has been granted the power to enforce these rights by issuing writs (Article 32) in the nature of Mandamus, Habeas Corpus, Prohibition, Certiorari and Quo Warranto. Even High Courts can also enforce these rights by issuing suitable writs (Article 226).

These rights are necessary for multi-facet development of a human being. The concept of Fundamental Right has been borrowed from Constitution of USA.

It must be noted that these Fundamental Rights are not absolute. Reasonable and justified restrictions can be imposed in the interest of public. The State has to balance the individual interest and social interest in securing welfare of the people.

1. Directive Principle of State Policy : These are contained in Part IV of the Constitution. They are not enforceable but they are fundamental to the governance of State. Though they are not enforceable, the State is expected to follow them to achieve the objectives of Welfare State. These are in the form of directives to the legislature and executive. Inspiration has been drawn from the Constitution of Republic of Ireland. Granville Austin has termed these principles as 'Soul of the State'. 26th and 42nd Constitutional Amendments gave

importance to Directive Principles over Fundamental Rights. Laws which implement Directive Principles of State Policy cannot be challenged in to court on the basis that they are Fundamental Rights conferred under the Article 14 & 19 of the Constitution.

2. Universal Adult Suffrage : Democratic government is people's government. The country is administered by the elected representatives of the people. The Constitution gives every person, above the age of 18 years, right to elect the representatives for the Parliament and State Legislature. This right is not qualified either on the basis of sex, property or taxation. The old system of communal electorates has been abolished. The Constitution (61th Amendment) Act 1989 amended Article 326 and reduced the age limit for adult suffrage to 18 years from 21 years.

3. Blend of rigidity and flexibility : Rigidity or flexibility of the Constitution depends upon the amendment process. Written Constitutions are generally considered to be rigid. A rigid Constitution requires special method of amendment while a flexible Constitution can be amendment by ordinary process of legislation. Although the Indian Constitution is written, yet it has a unique mixture of flexibility and rigidity. Only few provisions of the Constitution require the consent of half of the States. Rest provisions can be amended by special majority of Parliament.

4. Federal Constitution with centralizing tendency : This is one of the important features of the Constitution. It is a Federal Constitution but it acquires unitary tendency during the time of emergency. During proclamation of emergency the distribution of power between Centre and State undergoes a radical change. The Parliament

acquires the power to legislate on any subject mentioned in the State List. Executive and financial arrangements are also altered and Centre can direct State on these matters as well.

5. Independent Judiciary : Establishment of independent judiciary is the important feature of the Indian Constitution. Conferment of rights will have true effect if there is a sound mechanism for enforcement of such rights. Impartial judiciary with power of judicial review is essential for protection of rights. Supreme Court is considered to be a guardian of the Constitution.

6. Single Citizenship : Generally in a Federal Constitution there is a provision for dual citizenship i.e. citizenship of Centre and of State. American Constitution provides for dual citizenship. Case of Indian Constitution is different. Despite being a Federal Constitution it provides for a single citizenship. There is no separate citizenship for the States. This instills a sense of unity amongst the citizens despite having diversity in many spheres.

7. A Secular State : Preamble declares India to be a secular State. A secular State in case of religion is completely neutral. It treats all religions equally and does not discriminate on the basis of religion. Articles 25 to 28 also consolidate this aspect and give the right to every person to profess, practice and propagate religion.

Fundamental Duties : Fundamental Duties have been provided in Part IV-A (Article 51-A) of the Constitution. They have been added by 42nd Constitutional Amendment, 1976. The amendment added 10 fundamental duties which were increased to 11 by 86th Constitutional Amendment, 2002. It serves as a reminder to the citizens that they owe certain duties towards the nation apart from enjoying the rights conferred by the Constitution.

Difference between fundamental rights and directive principles

The Preamble of the Indian Constitution states that India is a sovereign, socialist, secular, and democratic republic. Being a democratic republic, India confers certain Fundamental Rights to its citizens and some rights to the non-citizens of the country. Fundamental Rights are the rights that are guaranteed by the Constitution of India to safeguard the interests of the people.

Directive Principles of State Policy (DPSP) are certain principles which are given to the institutes of the State in order to carry out effective governance of the country. Unlike, Fundamental Rights, Directive Principles are not enforceable by the courts of law. However, it does not imply that they do not have any significance; they are fundamental guidelines which the State should follow for effective governance.

Fundamental Rights

Fundamental Rights are guaranteed under Part III of the Constitution of India. Articles 12 to 35 of the Constitution of India deal with the various Fundamental Rights. Fundamental Rights are not absolute in nature (reasonable restrictions can be imposed), yet it is useful in providing justice to the people. The power of the rights can be gauzed by the fact that a person can directly approach the Supreme Court of India under Article 32 of the Constitution of India.

Origin of Fundamental Rights

In order to understand the needs of the Fundamental Rights, it is pertinent to understand its origin. The seed of Fundamental Rights was sown in the Swaraj Bill of 1895, which talked about the concept of Freedom of Speech, Right to Privacy and other such concepts. England Bill of Rights (1689), United States Bill of Rights (1791), and France Declaration of the Rights of Man (1789) were some of the concepts that gave inception to the thought of having Fundamental Rights in place.

The brutal acts committed by the Britishers under the Rowlatt Act, 1919; further paved the way for having Fundamental Rights to save the people from the injustice that was meted out to them. Further, the Nehru Commission of 1928 discussed the need of having certain rights which were deemed fundamental and people at the same time, were also intrigued by the independence of Ireland. The Directive Policy of Ireland particularly impressed people and they wanted whenever the self-government of India would be formed, they should follow in the footsteps of Ireland's directive policies.

Eventually, Fundamental Rights were incorporated in the first draft of the Constitution which was prepared by the Drafting Committee, whose chairman was Dr. B.R. Ambedkar. After the first draft, Fundamental Rights were included in the second and third drafts as well and finally into the present Constitution.

Rights provided under Part III of the Constitution

Right to Equality (Articles 14-18)

Articles 14 to 18 of the Constitution of India are all about the concept of the Right to Equality. Right to Equality means that everyone should be treated equally before the law thereby preventing discrimination on the grounds of caste, creed, religion, sex, and place of birth. The concept also talks about providing equal opportunity for employment to all people and abolishing untouchability and titles.

Right to Freedom (Articles 19-22)

Articles 19 to 22 give citizens the right to live their lives with dignity. Some of the basic rights such as Freedom of Speech and Expression, Freedom to Form Associations, etc; are essential in maintaining human dignity. These rights are consciously introduced in the Constitution to provide freedom to individuals which were curtailed in the pre-independence era.

Right against Exploitation (Articles 23-24)

Articles 23 and 24 of the Constitution prohibit human trafficking and sexual exploitation of women and children. Begar, slavery and any other form of forced labour is prohibited under the Constitution. Right against Exploitation also prohibits employment of children aged below 14 in hazardous activities; such as factories or mines.

Right to Freedom of Religion (Articles 25-28)

Right to Freedom of Religion is not only available to

individuals but also to religious groups. This Fundamental Right provides for freedom of practising religion to various religious groups and individuals. This guarantees the freedom of conscience, freedom to practice, profess and practice religion to all the citizens. The Article provides for a provision that the State can make laws in order to regulate and restrict any financial, economic, or secular activity in association with any religion. Under this Fundamental Right, religious institutions are allowed to form and maintain their religious institutions, they can acquire any moveable and immovable property and these properties must be administered in accordance with the law.

Cultural and Educational Rights (Articles 29-30)
This Fundamental Right has been exclusively included for linguistic and religious minorities in order to safeguard the interests of linguistic and religious minorities. India is known for its vast diversity and in order to protect it, it is pertinent to provide some safeguards to linguistic and religious minorities.

Cultural and Educational Rights provide an avenue for linguistic and religious minorities to protect, preserve and propagate their culture. The right provides that all religious and linguistic minorities can establish and administer the educational institutions and the State cannot deny admission to any individual on the basis of caste, creed, religion, etc.

Right to Constitutional Remedies (Article 32-35)
Right to Constitutional Remedies (Articles 32 to 35) empowers the citizens to move to a court of law in case of

any denial of the Fundamental Rights. For example: If any citizen is imprisoned, he has the right to move the court to ensure that imprisonment was made as per legal provision by lodging a Public Interest Litigation (PIL). If it comes out that the imprisonment was not as per the procedure established by law or was in contravention of any legal provision then the court can issue various kinds of writs in order to protect the citizen.

Directive Principles of State Policy

Directive Principles of State Policy (DPSP) are the principles or guidelines mentioned in Part IV of the Constitution. Directive Principles of State Policy of India have been adopted from the Irish Constitution, influenced by the Irish National Movement especially Irish Home Rule Movement. Articles 36-51 discuss various Directive Principles of State Policy. Directive Principles of State Policy, unlike Fundamental Rights, are not enforceable in a court of law, but that does not undermine their importance. Despite not being enforceable, DPSPs are extremely important as they give certain guidelines to the State for carrying out effective governance.

Directive Principles of State Policy are highly inspired by the concepts of social justice, foreign policy and economic welfare. The need for these principles in India stems from the fact that the people of the country were highly inspired by the independence of Ireland from the control of Britishers. The Indian people who were striving for independence looked up to Irish Constitution and they wanted to adopt a similar model of governance, once the country achieved independence. Looking at the diversity and vastness of India, people felt the Irish Constitution should be emulated in India as well because it comprehensively tackled social and economic challenges. DPSPs look for the welfare of the citizens by providing them with good social and economic conditions.

Significance of Directive Principles of State Policy

Directive Principles of State Policy strive to promote the social, and economic welfare of the individuals by securing social order. They work towards promoting the concepts of equality, liberty and justice which are enshrined in the Preamble of the Constitution. Swaying away from the colonial period, which was referred to as a "police state," to a modern "welfare state," where there is a social democracy.

Although DPSPs are not enforceable in a court of law, still they are instrumental in establishing the constitutional viability of a law. The Supreme Court has ruled that if a law is in question regarding its constitutional viability then if it seeks to give effect to Directive Principles of State Policy then the law might be held constitutional in relation to Article 14 of the Constitution.

Type of Directive Principles of State Policy

Articles 36-51 elucidate everything regarding the Directive Principles of State Policy. The essence of DPSPs is divided into four core principles:

1. Socialistic Principles

Socialistic principles are aimed at tackling complex social and economic issues and look to pave a model pathway toward a modern welfare state.

Article 38: Under Article 38 the aim is to secure a social order throughout the country by using tools of social, economic and political justice. Reducing income inequality, status imbalance and other social issues are at the core of this principle.

Article 39: This Article aims at securing adequate means of livelihood for the citizens by providing equitable material resources to everyone, and striving for equal work pay for both men and women. This DPSP is also beneficial in preventing the concentration of wealth and also looks for the healthy development of children. Article 39A gives out guidelines for promoting equal justice and providing free legal aid to the poor.

Article 41: Article 41 relates to the discussion regarding unemployment. The core value of this article is to provide the Right to Work, Right to Education and Right to Public Assistance in cases of unemployment, old age and sickness.

Article 42: This Article guides the State to make provisions regarding just and humane working conditions for workers. The Article extends such provisions for maternity relief as well.

Article 43: Like Articles 41, and 42; this Article also lays emphasis on workers. Under this article, the State is guided to give a decent living standard and social and cultural opportunities to workers. Article 43A seeks to increase the participation of workers in various industries.

Article 47: In its effort to further the cause of social justice, Article 47 talks about raising the levels of nutrition and the standard of public health.

2. Gandhian Principles

Principles under this part of Directive Principles of State Policy are dedicated to the 'Father of Nation' Mahatma

Gandhi. The principles mentioned in this Part are closely associated with Gandhian ideology that seeks a plan of reconstruction that Gandhiji has preached during the National Movement.

Article 40: Village panchayats have been touted as a self-government authority under the Article. The Article preaches that village panchayats should be given some powers to function as independent authorities.

Article 43: As was popular in the Gandhian era, the concept of promoting cottage industry, same has been iterated under Article 43 of the Directive Principles of State Policy. Article 43 B is all about promoting autonomous functioning, and professional management of cooperative societies.

Article 46: This Article is dedicated to weaker sections of the society or rather communities that have been through various oppressions. Educational and economic interests of SC, STs and other weaker sections have been propagated under the article. The State has been guided to ensure that there is no social injustice and exploitation against the weaker sections.

Article 47: The State should work to prohibit the consumption of intoxicating drinks and drugs which are harmful to health.

Article 48: Slaughtering of cattle should be prohibited and work should be done for improving their breeds.

3. Liberal Intellectual Principles

The ideology of liberalism has been reflected in the Liberal Intellectual Principles.

Article 44: A much talked and deliberated article is Article 44 of DPSP. Article 44 talks about Uniform Civil Code (UCC). Article 44 states that the State shall endeavour to secure a secure uniform civil code throughout the territory of India. Goa has often been referred to as a 'shining example' of the Uniform Civil Code, in fact, it is the only state in India that has UCC.

Article 45: This Article can be seen with reference to Article 21A. Article 45 states that the State should provide early childhood care and education to children up till they complete the age of fourteen years.

Article 48: Agriculture and animal husbandry shall be organised on the scientific lines.

Article 49: Monuments, places and objects of historic and artistic importance should be protected to conserve the heritage of the country.

Article 50: Article 50 is about the separation of the judiciary from the executive when it comes to the public service of the State.

Article 51: Under Article 51, international peace and security should be promoted; there should be an honourable relation between nations. International disputes should be settled by means of arbitration and there should be respect and obligation of international treaties.

Difference between fundamental rights and directive principles

1. Part in the Constitution in which they are mentioned
Fundamental Rights are mentioned in Part III of the Constitution while Directive Principles of State Policy are mentioned in Part IV of the Constitution. Articles 12-35 refer to Fundamental Rights while Article 36-51 refers to Directive Principles of State Policy.

2. Nature
Fundamental Rights in its essence are negative in nature

simply because they prohibit the State from taking any action which may violate the Fundamental Rights of the citizen. They are referred to as 'negative' because a claim made by an individual imposes a negative duty on all other people. For example: If the Right to Privacy is claimed by an individual, then it imposes a whole set of negative duties on all other individuals to not breach it.

Unlike Fundamental Rights, Directive Principles of State Policy are positive in nature as it requires the State to do certain things as opposed to restricting State. For example, under DPSPs, State has been suggested to enact a Uniform Civil Code throughout the country. This is positive in a sense as it allows the State to take certain actions.

3. Democracy type

Fundamental Rights ensure political democracy as they prevent the establishment of a despotic or an authoritarian government in the country and ensure that the liberties of people are protected from any invasion by the State.

Directive Principles of State Policy help in maintaining social and economic democracy as it ensures that the State shall maintain social order by promoting economic, social and political justice throughout the country.

4. Adaption Source

The Fundamental Rights of India have been adapted from the Constitution of the United States of America.

Directive Principles of State Policy have been highly inspired by the Irish Constitution. The independence of Ireland from the clutch of Britain highly motivated people to look up to the Irish Constitution for inspiration.

5. Consequences of violation

If the Fundamental Rights of an individual are violated then it is considered to be a punishable offence because Fundamental Rights are enforceable by law. Upon violation, legal proceedings can be initiated and punishment can be given as per provisions mentioned under the Indian laws.

Since Directive Principles of State Policy are not enforceable by law and are mere guidelines, their violation is not an offence and cannot be awarded punishment for their violation.

6. Touchstone for laws

If a law is passed by the Parliament, such that it tends to violate certain aspects of Fundamental Rights, High Courts and Supreme Court in such cases can declare these kinds of laws or amendments as unconstitutional.

Any law or amendment made or initiated by the Parliament that does not adhere to the guidelines mentioned in DPSPs, in such cases High Courts and Supreme Court do not hold power to declare these laws as unconstitutional.

7. Individualistic or collective

Fundamental Rights are individualistic in nature as they are instrumental in preserving the rights and welfare of citizens in an individualistic manner. For example; if the Right to Freedom of Speech of an individual is curbed; Constitution ensures that such right is made available to the aggrieved person.

Directive Principles of State Policy are more collective in nature because DPSP focuses on promoting the welfare of the entire society or community of the country in a collective manner. For example, under DPSP; State has been suggested to employ village panchayats as a self-governing authority to look after the welfare of people in toto.

8. Suspension

Fundamental Rights can be suspended only in case of Emergency under Article 359 of the Constitution by the

President. However, Fundamental Rights which are mentioned in Articles 20 and 21 cannot be suspended even during an emergency.

Directive Principles of State Policy can never be suspended, even during an emergency.

Conclusion

If we look at both Fundamental Rights and Directive Principles of State Policy, both have been extremely instrumental in the governance of the country ever since the independence of India. The concept of Fundamental Right in the United States of America and Directive Principles from the Constitution of Ireland has been borrowed in true essence. Both have served well in the governance of the country but when we compare both of them hand in hand Directive Principles of State Policy falls short in comparison to Fundamental Rights.

While Fundamental Right is more objective and has more imposing value, Directive Principles of State Policy in some ways are subjective because it is a kind of moral obligation which the State may or may not implement up to their discretion. Fundamental Rights are aimed at empowering people as it prohibits the State from taking extreme steps which is necessary for a democracy to survive.

On the other hand, Directive Principles of State Policy empowers the State to take action for the welfare of the country which is needed because India is a vast country and it is extremely pertinent to maintain social, economic and political justice throughout the country. Despite differences, both cannot be seen as exclusive from each other; rather they should complement each other for effective governance of the country.

Important Questions and Answers

1. Under which part of the Constitution, Fundamental Rights are mentioned?

Ans. Fundamental Rights are mentioned under Part III of the Constitution of India.

2. Which part of the Constitution deals with Directive Principles of State Policy?

Ans. Directive Principles of State Policy are mentioned under Part IV of the Constitution of India.

3. From which country's Constitution, Fundamental Rights and Directive Principles of State Policy have been borrowed?

Ans. Fundamental Rights are borrowed from the Constitution of the USA, while Directive Principles of State Policy have been borrowed from the Irish Constitution.

4. What are the six types of Fundamental Rights mentioned in part III of the Constitution?

Ans. i. Right to Equality. ii. Right to Freedom. iii. Right against Exploitation. iv. Right to Freedom of Religion. v. Cultural and Educational Rights. vi. Right to Constitutional Remedies.

5. Are Fundamental Rights and Directive Principles of State Policy enforceable?

Ans. Fundamental Rights are enforceable but Directive Principles of State Policy are not enforceable.

6. Why are Fundamental Rights important?

Ans. Fundamental Rights are important because they protect the freedom and liberties of citizens against the State.

7. What is the role of Directive Principles of State Policy?

Ans. Directive Principles of State Policy provide guidelines to the State for effective governance of the country.

8. What is Uniform Civil Code?

Ans. Uniform Civil Code calls for the formulation and implementation of personal laws which would be followed by all the religious communities.

CHAPTER III

Institutional Functioning: Prime Minister, Parliament and Judiciary

Introduction

The term legislature has been derived from the Latin word *lex*, which means a distinct kind of legal rule mainly of general application. This rule is named legislation, and the institution, which enacts it on behalf of the people, is known as legislature. Essentially, there are two models of legislative structure: the Parliamentary and the Presidential. In the parliamentary model, the executive is selected by the legislature from among its own members. Therefore, the executive is responsible to the legislature. The Presidential system is based on the theory of separation of powers and does not permit any person to serve simultaneously in both executive and legislature.

The Parliament of India, which is the creation of the Constitution, is the supreme representative authority of the people. It is the highest legislative organ.

It is the national forum for the articulation of public opinion.

Indian Legislature: Historical Background

Indian Parliament did not emerge overnight; it evolved gradually during the British rule, particularly since 1858 when the British Crown assumed sovereignty over India from the East India Company. By the Government of India Act of 1858, the powers of the Crown were to be exercised by the Secretary of State for India assisted by a Council of India. The Secretary of State, who was responsible to the British Parliament, governed India through the Governor General, assisted by an Executive Council consisting of high government officials. There was no separation of powers; all the powers - legislative, executive, military and civil - were vested in this Governor General in Council.

The Indian Council Act of 1861 introduced little bit of popular element as it included some additional *non-official* members in the Executive Council and allowed them to participate in the transaction of legislative business. The Legislative Council was neither deliberative nor representative. Its members were nominated and their role was limited only to the consideration of legislative proposals placed by the Governor General.

Indian Councils Act of 1892 made two important improvements. First, non-official members of the Indian Legislative Council were henceforth to be nominated by the Bengal Chamber of Commerce and the Provincial Legislative Councils, while the non-official members of the Provincial Councils were to be nominated by certain local bodies such as universities, district boards, municipalities. Secondly, the Councils were empowered to discuss the budget and address questions to the Executive.

Indian Councils Act of 1909, based on Morley-Minto Reforms, for the first time, introduced both representative as well as popular features. At the Centre, election was introduced in the Legislative Council though the officials still retained the majority. But in the Provinces, the size of the Provincial Legislative Council was increased by including elected non-official members so that the officials no longer constituted the majority. This Act enhanced the deliberative functions of the Legislative Councils and provided them opportunity to move resolutions on the Budget and any other matter of public interest barring certain specified subjects, such as the Armed Forces, Foreign Affairs and the India States. The Government of India Act of 1915 consolidated all the previous Acts so that the executive, legislative and judicial functions could be derived from a single Act.

The next phase of legislative reforms emerged out of the Government of India Act of 1919 brought further legislative reforms in the form of responsible government in the Provinces. At the Centre, the legislature was made bicameral and elected majority was introduced in both the Houses. However, no element of responsible government was introduced at the Centre. The Governor General in Council continued to be responsible as before to the British Parliament through the Secretary of State.

The Government of India Act of 1935 came into being after several parleys between the Indian national leaders and Britain. It contemplated a federation consisting of British Indian Provinces and native states. It introduced bicameral legislatures in six Provinces. It demarcated legislative power of the Centre and the Provinces through three lists: the Central List, the Provincial List and the Concurrent List. However, the Central Executive was not made responsible to the legislature. The Governor General as well as the Crown could veto bills passed by the Central Legislature. The Governor-General besides the Ordinance-making powers had independent powers of legislation or permanent Acts. Similar limitations existed in case of Provincial Legislatures existed as well.

The international political scene and the conditions in India and Britain led the British government to an unequivocal acceptance of India's claim to freedom. The

Indian Independence Act of 1947 was passed setting up two independent dominions, India and Pakistan. The legislature of each dominion was to have full legislative sovereignty. The powers of the legislature of the dominion were exercisable without any limitations whatsoever by the Constituent Assembly formed in 1946. This Constituent Assembly adopted the Constitution of India, which received the signature of the President on 26th November 1950.

Union Legislature

Under the provision of Article 79, the Parliament of India consists of the President and the two Houses - the Lower House or Lok Sabha (House of the People) and the Upper House or Rajya Sabha (Council of States). While the Lok Sabha is subject to dissolution, the Rajya Sabha is a permanent chamber which cannot be dissolved. The office of the President also never remains vacant.

The President

While the American President is not a part of the Legislature (Congress), the President of India is an integral part of the Indian Parliament. However, he cannot sit and participate in the deliberations in any of the two Houses.

The President of India performs certain important role vis-à-vis the Parliament. The President summons and prorogues the House from one session to another and has the power to dissolve the Lok Sabha. No bill passed by both the Houses can become a law without the President's assent. Further certain bills can be introduced only after the recommendation of the President has been obtained.

The President also has the power to promulgate Ordinances when both the Houses are not in session. These Ordinances, though temporary in nature, have the same force and power as a law passed by Parliament.

The Lok Sabha

The Lower House or the House of the People is popularly known as Lok Sabha. Its members are directly elected by the people. The maximum number of members to be elected which was fixed by the Constitution at 500. It was raised to 520 members by the Seventh Constitutional Amendment (1956) and to 545 members by the 42nd Constitutional Amendment (1976). This includes not more than 525 members chosen by direct election from territorial constituencies in the States and not more 20 members to represent the Union Territories. In addition, the President may nominate two members of the Anglo-Indian community if he is of the opinion that the community is not adequately represented in the Lok Sabha.

The distribution of seats among the States is based on the principle of territorial representation which means each State is allotted seats on the basis of its population in proportion to the total population of all the States. For election purpose, each state is divided into territorial units called constituencies which are more or less of the same size with regard to the population.

The election to the Lok Sabha is conducted on the basis of adult franchise; every adult who has attained 18 years of age is eligible to vote. The candidate who secures the largest number of votes gets elected. The Constitution provides for an independent organisation known as the Election Commission to conduct elections. The normal life of the

Lower House is five years, though it can be dissolved earlier by the President.

To be a member of the Lok Sabha, a person should be an Indian citizen, must have completed 25 years of age and must possess all other qualifications that are prescribed by a law of the Parliament. A candidate seeking election to the Lok Sabha can contest from any parliamentary constituency from any of the States in India.

The Constitution has laid down certain disqualifications for membership. No person can be member of both Houses of Parliament or member both of Parliament and of a State legislature. The candidate may contest from several seats, but if elected from more than one, he has to vacate all expect one according to his choice. If a person is elected both to the State legislature and the Parliament and if he does not resign from the State legislature within the specified time period, he will forfeit his seat in Parliament. A member should not hold any office of profit under the Central or State government except those that are exempted by a law of Parliament, and should not have been declared as an insolvent or of unsound mind by a competent court. A member also gets disqualified when he remains absent from the meetings of the House for a period of sixty days without prior permission or when he voluntarily acquires the citizenship of another country or is under any acknowledgement of allegiance to a foreign state.

The Rajya Sabha

The Rajya Sabha or Council of States consists of not more than 250 members of which 12 members are nominated by the President from amongst persons having 'special knowledge or practical experience in literature, science, art, and social service.' The remaining members are elected by the members of the State Legislative Assemblies in accordance with the system of proportional representation by means of single transferable vote. Thus, unlike Lok Sabha, Rajya Sabha adopts the method of indirect election. For the purpose of this election, each State is allotted a number of seats, mainly on the basis of their population. The Rajya Sabha, thus reflects the federal character by representing the States or the units of the federation. However, it does not follow the American principle of equality of State representation in the Second Chamber. Whereas every State of the United States sends two representatives to the Senate, in India, the number of representatives of the States to the Rajya Sabha varies from one (Nagaland) to 34 (Uttar Pradesh) depending upon the population of a state.

Rajya Sabha is a continuing chamber as it is a permanent body not subject to dissolution. One third of its members retire at the end of every two years and elections are held for the vacant positions. A member of Rajya Sabha has a six year term, unless he resigns or is disqualified.

Special Powers of Rajya Sabha:

The Rajya Sabha has hardly any control over the ministers who are individually and jointly responsible to the Lok Sabha. Though it has every right to seek information on all matters which are exclusively in the domain of Lok Sabha, it has no power to pass a vote of no-confidence in the Council of Ministers. Moreover, the Rajya Sabha has not much say in matters of money bills. Nevertheless, the Constitution grants certain special powers to the Rajya Sabha. As the sole representative of the

States, the Rajya Sabha enjoys two exclusive powers which are of considerable importance.

First, under Article 249, the Rajya Sabha has the power to declare that, in the national interest, the Parliament should make laws with respect to a matter enumerated in the State List. If by a two-thirds majority, Rajya Sabha passes a resolution to this effect, the Union Parliament can make laws for the whole or any part of India for a period of one year.

The second exclusive power of the Rajya Sabha is with regard to the setting up of All-India Services. If the Rajya Sabha passes a resolution by not less than two-thirds of the members present and voting, the parliament is empowered to make laws providing for creation of one or more All-India Services common to the Union and the Sates.

Thus, these special provisions make the Rajya Sabha an important component of Indian Legislature rather than just being an ornamental second chamber like the House of Lords of England. The constitution makers have designed it not just to check any hasty legislation, but also to play the role of an important influential advisor. Its compact composition and permanent character provides it continuity and stability. As many of its members are "elder statesmen" the Rajya Sabha commands respectability.

Presiding Officers

Each house of Parliament has it own presiding officers. The Lok Sabha has a Speaker as its principal presiding officer and a deputy speaker to assist him and officiates as presiding officer in his absence. The Rajya Sabha is presided over by the Chairperson, assisted by a deputy chairperson. The latter performs all the duties and functions of the former in case of his/her absence.

The Speaker

The position of the Speaker of the Lok Sabha is more or less similar to the Speaker of the English House of Commons. The office of the Speaker is symbol of high dignity and authority. Once elected to the office, the speaker severs his party affiliation and starts functioning in an impartial manner. He acts as the guardian of the rights and privileges of the members.

The Speaker is conferred with a number of powers to ensure an orderly and efficient conduct of the business of the House. He conducts the proceedings of the house, maintains order and decorum in the house and decides points of order, interprets and applies rules of the house. The Speaker's decision is final in all such matters. The Speaker certifies whether a bill is money bill or not and his decision is final. The Speaker authenticates that the house has passed the bill before it is presented to the other house or the President of India for his assent. The Speaker in consultation with the leader of the house determines the order of business. He decides on the admissibility of questions, motions and resolutions. The Speaker will not vote in the first instance, but can exercise a casting vote in case of a tie. The Speaker appoints the chairpersons of all the Committees of the house and exercises control over the Secretarial staff of the house.

The Speakers conduct cannot be discusses in in the house except in a substantive motion. His salary and allowances are charged to the Consolidated Fund of India so that the independent character of the office is maintained.

A special feature of the Speaker's office is that even when the House is dissolved, the Speaker does not vacate his office. He continues in office until the new House elects another Speaker. In the absence of the Speaker, the Deputy Speaker presides over the House.

Chairperson of Rajya Sabha

The Vice-President of India is the ex-officio chairperson of the Rajya Sabha; but during any period when the Vice President acts a President or discharges the functions of the President, he does not perform the duties as a presiding officer of the Rajya Sabha. The Vice-President is elected by the members of both the houses of Parliament assembled at a joint meeting, in accordance with the system of proportional representation by means of single transferable vote and the voting at such elections is by secret ballot. The Vice President is not a member of either house of Parliament or of a house of legislature of any State. He holds office for a term of five years from the date on which he enters upon his office or until he resigns his office or is removed from his office by a resolution passed by a majority of members of the Rajya Sabha and agreed to by the Lok Sabha. The functions and duties of the Chairperson of the Rajya Sabha are the same as those of the Speaker of the Lok Sabha.

Legislative Procedure

Law making is the primary function of the legislature. As modern society is very complex in nature, law making also becomes a complex process. The Constitution of India prescribes the following stages of legislative procedure.

The first stage of legislation is introduction of a bill which embodies the proposed law and is accompanied by the "Statement of Objects and Reasons". The introduction of the bill is also called the first reading of the bill. There are two types of bills: ordinary bills and money bills. A bill other than money or financial bill may be introduced in either House of Parliament and requires passage in both the Houses before it can be presented for the President's assent. A bill may be introduced either by a Minister or a private member. Every bill that is introduced in the House has to be published in the Gazette. Normally, there is no debate at the time of introduction of a bill. The member who introduces the bill may make a brief statement indicating broadly the aims and objects of the bill. If the bill is opposed at this stage, one of the members opposing the bill may be permitted to give his reasons. After this the question is put to vote. If the House is in favour of the introduction of the bill, then it goes to the next stage.

In the second stage, there are four alternative courses. After its introduction, a bill (I) may be taken into consideration; (II) may be referred to a Select Committee of the House; (III) may be referred to a Joint Committee of both the Houses; (IV) may be circulated for the purpose of soliciting public opinion. While the first three options are generally adopted in case of routine legislation, the last option is resorted to only when the proposed legislation is likely to arouse public controversy and agitation.

The day one of these motions is carried out, the principles of the bill and its general provisions may be discussed. If the bill is taken into consideration, Amendments to the bill and clause by clause consideration of the provisions of the bill is undertaken. If the bill is referred to the Select Committee of the House, it considers the bill and submits its report to the House. Then the clauses of the bill are open to consideration and amendments are admissible. This is the most time-consuming stage. Once the clause by clause consideration is over and every clause is voted, the second reading of the bill comes to an end.

In the third stage the member in charge moves that "the bill be passed". At the third reading, the progress of the bill is quick as normally only verbal or purely formal amendments are moved and discussion is very brief. Once all the amendments are disposed off, the bill is finally passed in the House where it was introduced. Thereafter, it is transmitted to the other House for its consideration.

When the bill comes up for considered by the other House, it has to undergo all the stages as in the originating House. There are three options before the House (I) it may finally pass the bill as sent by the originating House; (II) it may reject the bill altogether or amend it and return to the originating House; (III) it may not take any action on the bill and if more than six months pass after the date of receipt of the bill, this means rejection.

The originating House now considers the returned bill in the light of the amendments. If it accepts these amendments, it sends a message to the other House to this effect. If it does not accept these amendments, then the bill is returned to the other House with a message to that effect. In case both the Houses do not come to an agreement, the President convenes a joint-sitting of the two Houses. The disputed provision is finally adopted or rejected by a simple majority of vote of those who are present and voting.

A bill that is finally passed by both the Houses is presented with the signature of the Speaker to the President for his assent. This is normally the last stage. If the President gives the assent, the bill becomes an Act and is placed in the Statute Book. If the President withholds his assent, there is an end to the bill. The President may also return the bill for the reconsideration of the Houses with a message requesting them to reconsider it. If, however, the Houses pass the bill again with or without amendments and the bill is presented to the President for his assent for the second time, the President has no power to withhold his assent.

Thus, law-making is a long, cumbersome and time-consuming process; it becomes difficult to pass a bill within a short time. Proper drafting of the bill saves time and skillful soliciting of opposition support makes the task easier.

Money Bills

Financial bill may be said to be any bill which relates to revenue and expenditure. But the financial bill is not a money bill. Art. 110 states that no bill is a money bill unless it is certified by the Speaker of the Lok Sabha. A money bill cannot be introduced in the Rajya Sabha. Once a money bill is passed by the Lok Sabha, it is transmitted to the Rajya Sabha. The Rajya Sabha cannot reject a money bill. It must, within a period of fourteen days from the date of receipt of the bill, return the bill to the Lok Sabha which may thereupon either accept or reject all or any of the recommendations. If the Lok Sabha accepts any of the recommendations, the money bill is deemed to have been passed by both Houses. Even if the Lok Sabha does not accept any of the recommendations, the money bill is deemed to have been passed by both the Houses without any amendments. If a money bill passed by the Lok Sabha and transmitted to the Rajya Sabha for its recommendations is not returned to it within fourteen days, it is deemed to have been passed by both the Houses at the expiry of the said period in the original form.

Parliamentary Priviledges

For free and efficient functioning of the members of Parliament it is important that they are granted some privileges. There are two types of privileges for the members of Parliament: enumerated and unenumerated. The important privileges a member enjoys under the enumerated category are : i) Freedom of speech in each House of the parliament; ii) Immunity from proceedings in any Court in respect of anything said or any vote cast; iii) Immunity of liability in respect of publication by or under the authority of either house of Parliament of any report, paper, votes or proceedings; iv) Freedom from arrest in civil cases for duration of the session for a period of 40 days before and after the session; and v) Exemption from attending as a witness in a Court.

In the unenumerated category fall similar privileges and immunities which are granted to the members of the House of Commons of British Parliament. Like the House of Commons, the Indian Parliament has power to punish a person, whether a member or a non-member, in case of contempt of Parliament.

Parliamentary Devices to Control the Executive

As observed, one of the important functions of the Parliament is to control the executive. A number of mechanisms are available to it for this purpose.

The rules of procedure and conduct of business in parliament provide that unless the presiding officers otherwise direct, every sitting begins with the Question Hour, which is available for asking and answering questions. Asking of questions is an inherent parliamentary right of all the members, irrespective of their party affiliations. The real object of the member in asking the question is to point out the shortcomings of the administration, to ascertain the thinking of the government in formulating its policy and where the policy already exists, in making suitable modifications in that policy.

In case the answer given to a question does not satisfy the member who raised it and if he feels the need for detailed 'explanation in public interest' he may request the presiding officer for a discussion. The presiding office can allow discussion, usually in the last half an hour of a sitting.

Members can, with the prior permission of the presiding officer, call the attention of a Minister to any matter of public importance and request the Minister to make a statement on the subject. The Minister may either make a brief statement immediately or may ask for time to make the statement at a later hour or date.

Members can take the government to task for a recent act of omission or commission having serious consequence by resorting to adjournment motion. This motion is intended to draw the attention of the house to a recent matter of urgent public importance having serious consequences for the country and in regard to which a motion or a resolution in the proper notice will be too late. Adjournment motion is an extraordinary procedure which, if admitted, leads to setting aside the normal business of the house for discussing a definite matter of public importance. Adoption of an adjournment motion amounts to the censure of the government.

Besides these devices, Parliament exercises control over the executive through various house committees.

Parliamentary Committees

The accountability of the executive to the Parliament and the Parliament's right to oversee and scrutinise the way in which the executive functions are accepted as axiomatic. But in practice due to some unavoidable factors, such as the pressure on Parliament and its operational procedures, it is difficult for parliament as a body to undertake thorough scrutiny of the multifaceted and complex details of day to day administration and its financial transactions.

Parliament has solved the problem by establishing a series of committees with necessary powers to scrutinise the working of the different departments of the government.

Among the important Committees, which scrutinise the government's works, particularly in the area of public finances, two committees need special mention: Public Accounts Committee and Estimates Committee. These and other Committees are expected to keep the executive on its toes. They ensure an effective and comprehensive examination of all the proposed policies. Often, Committees provides an ideal context for discussing controversial and sensitive matters in a non-partisan manner, away the glare of publicity. They provide a useful forum for the utilisation of experience and ability that may otherwise remain untapped. They also constitute a valuable training ground for future ministers and presiding officers.

State Legislature

In most respects, state legislatures are similar to the Parliament of India. However, the choice of unicameralism or bicameralism was left to the states, depending on how they weighed the functions of the second chamber compared to the costs involved in running it. Very few states have opted to have bicameral legislature consisting of the Legislative Assembly (Vidhan Sabha) and the Legislative Council (Vidhan Parishad).

The Legislative Assembly of each State is composed of members chosen by direct election on the basis of adult suffrage from territorial constituencies. The size of the Assembly varies from a minimum of 40 to no more than 500. The duration of the Legislative Assembly is for five years.

The membership of the Legislative Council shall not be less than 40 but not more than one-third of the total membership of the Assembly. The House is composed of partly elected and partly nominated members. Normally, 1/6 of total members are nominated by the Governor and the rest are indirectly elected on a complicated formula involving graduates, educators and members of the Assembly.

The position of the Council is inferior to that of the Assembly so much so that it may well be considered as unnecessary. A) The very nature of composition of the Legislative Council makes its position weak, being partly elected and partly nominated, and representing various interests. B) Its survival depends on the will of the Assembly, as the latter has the power to abolish the Second Chamber by passing a resolution. C) The Council of Ministers are responsible only to the Assembly and not to the Council. D) As regard any ordinary bill originating in the Assembly, the Council's position is very weak for it can only delay its passage for a limited period. Hence, the second chamber of the State legislature is not a revising body, but a mere dilatory body.

The legislative process in the State Assembly is similar to that in the Parliament with one significant exception. The Governor can reserve any bill passed by the State legislature for the consideration of the President. Particularly in one case, it is obligatory on the Governor to reserve the bill, i.e., when the bill is derogatory to the powers of the High Court. If the President directs the Governor to return the bill for reconsideration, the Legislature must reconsider the bill within six months and if it is passed again, the bill is presented to the President again. But it shall not be obligatory on the President to give his assent. Thus, it is clear that once the Governor reserves a bill for the President, its subsequent enactment remains with the President and the Governor has no further role in it. Since the Constitution does not put any time limit upon the President either to declare his assent or withhold, the President can keep the bill in cold storage for an indefinite period without revealing his intention.

Decline of Legislature:

At present there exists a strong tendency indicating decline of legislature and corresponding enhancement of power of the executive. Several factors have contributed to this decline of the prestige and functioning of the Parliament.

Parliament is simply not able to devote its entire time to the details of the legislative measures. It could at best lay down broad policy and leave the rest to be taken up by the executive. Hence all bills contain a clause empowering the government to frame necessary regulations and bye laws. Thus, delegated legislation robs the Parliament to a great extent, the law making power, resulting in the decline in the prestige of the Parliament.

The ever-changing political and moral conditions in India are also responsible for the decline of the prestige of the Parliament. Dominance by the party, the lack of party organisation, the malaise of political defections, corruption and the decline of the morale of politician have all contributed to the erosion of the prestige of the Parliament. A major threat to Parliament in India is posed by the growth of diverse and divisive forces in all the political parties. Both the ruling and opposition parties are prompted more by considerations of expediency and political motives than ideology. The ineffectiveness of the opposition and the lack of a strongly articulated public opinion have added to the erosion of Parliaments position vis a vis the executive headed by the Prime Minister. In theory, we have a parliamentary system where the executive is controlled by the legislature, but in reality, the powers of the legislature have passed into the hands of the executive.

Conclusion

The Parliament of India, the supreme legislative organ in the country, has a long historical background. While legislature in some form came into being during the days of the East India Company, it was only when the Company rule was replaced by that of the Crown that the powers of the Union Legislature as well as its democratic base began to gradually grown.

The Parliament consists of the President, the Lok Sabha and the Rajya Sabha. To get elected to the Parliament, one has to fulfil certain qualifications prescribed by the Constitution and the Parliament. Members of the Parliament have certain privileges to enable them to function better. Each house has its own presiding officer to conduct the meetings of the House and to protect the dignity and honour of the House.

The primary function of the Parliament is to enact laws. In addition, it holds the Council of Ministers responsible for its policies and criticises the policies wherever necessary. It also has the powers to amend the constitution and to impeach the President. There are several Committees appointed from among its members for effective functioning. Devices like the question hour, adjournment motion, calling attention motion, etc. are available for Parliament to check the government. Passing of the budget, an important function of the Parliament, provides it with an opportunity to scrutinise the activities of the government.

There is a declining trend in the position of the legislature all over the world. Delegated legislation, ascendancy of the executive over the other organs of the government, emergence of strong party system, etc. are some of the reasons for such a trend. Despite these trends, the Parliament still commands respect and is able to maintain its position vis a vis the other organs of the government.

Judiciary: Structure, Organization and Functioning

Judiciary, legislature and executive are the three branches of the State. In India, we have an independent judiciary. The other organs of the government cannot interfere with the functioning of the judiciary.

Judiciary

The judiciary is that branch of the government that interprets law, settles disputes and administers justice to all citizens. The judiciary is considered the watchdog of democracy, and also the guardian of the Constitution. For democracy to function effectively, it is imperative to have an impartial and independent judiciary.

Independent Judiciary

What is the meaning of independent judiciary?

(i) It means that the other branches of the government, namely, the executive and the legislature, does not interfere with the judiciary's functioning.

(ii) The judiciary's decision is respected and not interfered with by the other organs.

(iii) It also means that judges can perform their duties without fear or favour.

Independence of the judiciary also does not mean that the judiciary functions arbitrarily and without any accountability. It is accountable to the Constitution of the country.

How is the Judiciary's independence provided for?

The Constitution provides for a number of provisions that ensure that the independence of the judiciary is maintained and protected.

Judiciary Structure

India has a single integrated judicial system. The judiciary in India has a pyramidal structure with the Supreme Court (SC) at the top. High Courts are below the SC, and below them are the district and subordinate courts. The lower courts function under the direct superintendence of the higher courts.

Apart from the above structure, there are also two branches of the legal system, which are:

1. **Criminal Law:** These deal with the committing of a crime by any citizen/entity. A criminal case starts when the local police files a crime report. The court finally decides on the matter.
2. **Civil Law:** These deal with disputes over the violation of the Fundamental Rights of a citizen.

The SC has three types of jurisdictions. They are original, appellate and advisory. The jurisdiction of the Supreme Court are mentioned in Articles 131, 133, 136 and 143 of the Constitution.

Functions of Judiciary

The functions of the judiciary in India are:

1. **Administration of justice:** The chief function of the judiciary is to apply the law to specific cases or in settling disputes. When a dispute is brought before the courts it 'determines the facts' involved through

evidence presented by the contestants. The law then proceeds to decide what law is applicable to the case and applies it. If someone is found guilty of violating the law in the course of the trial, the court will impose a penalty on the guilty person.

2. **Creation of judge-case law:** In many cases, the judges are not able to, or find it difficult to select the appropriate law for application. In such cases, the judges decide what the appropriate law is on the basis of their wisdom and common sense. In doing so, judges have built up a great body of 'judge-made law' or 'case law.' As per the doctrine of 'stare decisis', the previous decisions of judges are generally regarded as binding on later judges in similar cases.

3. **Guardian of the Constitution:** The highest court in India, the SC, acts as the guardian of the Constitution. The conflicts of jurisdiction between the central government and the state governments or between the legislature and the executive are decided by the court. Any law or executive order which violates any provision of the constitution is declared unconstitutional or null and void by the judiciary. This is called 'judicial review.' Judicial review has the merit of guaranteeing the fundamental rights of individuals and ensuring a balance between the union and the units in a federal state.

4. **Protector of Fundamental Rights:** The judiciary ensures that people's rights are not trampled upon by the State or any other agency. The superior courts enforce Fundamental Rights by issuing writs.

5. **Supervisory functions:** The higher courts also perform the function of supervising the subordinate courts in India.

6. **Advisory functions:** The SC in India performs an advisory function as well. It can give its advisory opinions on constitutional questions. This is done in the absence of disputes and when the executive so desires.

7. **Administrative functions:** Some functions of the courts are non-judicial or administrative in nature. The courts may grant certain licenses, administer the estates (property) of deceased persons and appoint receivers. They register marriages, appoint guardians of minor children and lunatics.

8. **Special role in a federation:** In a federal system like India's, the judiciary also performs the important task of settling disputes between the centre and states. It also acts as an arbiter of disputes between states.

9. **Conducting judicial enquiries:** Judges normally are called to head commissions that enquire into cases of errors or omissions on the part of public servants.

Civil Courts

Civil courts deal with civil cases. Civil law is referred to in almost all cases other than criminal cases. Criminal law applies when a crime such as robbery, murder, arson, etc. is perpetrated.

- Civil law is applied in disputes when one person sues another person or entity. Examples of civil cases include divorce, eviction, consumer problems, debt or bankruptcy, etc.
- Judges in civil courts and criminal courts have different powers. While a judge in a criminal court can punish the convicted person by sending him/her to jail, a judge in a

civil court can make the guilty pay fines, etc.

- District Judges sitting in District Courts and Magistrates of Second Class and Civil Judge (Junior Division) are at the bottom of the judicial hierarchy in India.
- The court of the district judges is the highest civil court in a district.
- It has both administrative and judicial powers.
- The court of the District Judge is in the district HQ.
- It can try criminal and civil cases and hence, the judge is called District and Sessions Judge.
- Under the district courts, there are courts of the Sub-Judge, Additional Sub-Judge and Munsif Courts.
- Most civil cases are filed in the Munsif's court.

Civil courts have four types of jurisdiction:

- **Subject Matter Jurisdiction:** It can try cases of a particular type and relating to a particular subject.
- **Territorial Jurisdiction:** It can try cases within its geographical limit, and not beyond the territory.
- **Pecuniary Jurisdiction:** Cases related to money matters, suits of monetary value.
- **Appellate Jurisdiction:** This is the authority of a court to hear appeals or review a case that has already been decided by a lower court. The Supreme Court and the High Courts have appellate jurisdiction to hear cases that were decided by a lower court.

Important Questions and Answers

What is Article 124 A of Indian Constitution?

This article talks about the establishment and constitution of the Supreme Court.

What is the structure of Indian judiciary?

Judiciary in India has a pyramidal structure with the Supreme Court at the top.

What is obiter dictum in law?

Obiter dictum is an opinion or a remark made by a judge which does not form a necessary part of the court's decision.

What are the main function of judiciary?

The main function of the judiciary is to interpret and apply laws to cases.

Prime Minister and Council of Ministers

There is no direct election to the post of the **Prime Minister**. The President appoints the Prime Minister.

- The President appoints the leader of the majority party or the coalition of parties that commands a majority in the Lok Sabha, as Prime Minister.
- In case no single party or alliance gets a majority, the President appoints the person most likely to secure majority support.
- The Prime Minister does not have a fixed tenure. He continues in power so long as he remains the leader of the majority party or coalition.

After the appointment of the Prime Minister, the President appoints other ministers on the advice of the Prime Minister which are usually from the majority party or the coalition that has the majority in the Lok Sabha.

- The Prime Minister is free to choose ministers, as long as they are members of Parliament.
- A person who is not a member of Parliament can also become a minister. But such a person has to get elected to one of the Houses of Parliament within six months of appointment as minister.

The Council of Ministers is the official name for the body that includes all the Ministers. It usually has 60 to 80 Ministers of different ranks as mentioned below:

1. **Cabinet Ministers** are usually top level leaders of the ruling party or parties who are in charge of the major ministries. The cabinet is the inner ring of the Council of Ministers and comprises about 25 ministers.
2. **Ministers of State with independent charge** are usually in-charge of smaller Ministries. They participate in the Cabinet meetings only when specially invited.
3. **Ministers of State** are the junior ministers, who are assigned to assist cabinet ministers and the ministers of state with independent charge.

Parliamentary democracy in most countries is often known as the Cabinet form of government because most of the decisions are taken in Cabinet meetings. Every ministry has secretaries, who are civil servants. The secretaries provide the necessary background information to the ministers to take decisions. The Cabinet as a team is assisted by the Cabinet Secretariat.

Powers of the Prime Minister

As head of the government, the Prime Minister has wide-ranging powers, which are mentioned below:

1. The Prime Minister chairs Cabinet meetings. He is the head of the government.
2. He coordinates the work of different Departments.
3. His decisions are final in case disagreements arise between Departments.
4. He exercises general supervision of different ministries.
5. All ministers work under his leadership.
6. The Prime Minister distributes and redistributes work to the ministers.
7. He has the power to dismiss ministers.
8. When the Prime Minister quits, the entire ministry quits.

CHAPTER IV

Power Structure in India: Caste, class and patriarchy

Introduction

In order to get understanding regarding the Indian politics, first of all, we need to understand the power-structure in India i.e., Caste, class, patriarchy. All these are inherited in traditions of India for long span of time. Thus, it becomes necessary to understand these structures in our society and how it is interpreted by many scholars over the time and how is it functioning with the changing scenario of social-economic-political milieu. We need to understand the emerging politics in relations with these tenets to understand the converted Indian politics. In this chapter, we analyze the power structure in India in terms of caste and its relationship with politics and will interpret that how caste politics have been an important and inalienable part of Indian government and politics.

Prior to the government of India act, 1935, the "schedule" caste was classified as the 'depressed classes'. "This social group is categorized amongst the poorest and most subordinated in terms of human development in Indian society. In five states of India i.e. UP, West Bengal, Bihar, Tamil Nadu and Andhra Pradesh, more than half of SC population is concentrated. The historical processes of economic and social exclusion, and discrimination based on caste are responsible for the depreciation of this group". "Schedule" refers to a schedule to the Constitution, and "scheduled caste" belongs to such castes, races, "tribes, or parts of groups within castes, races, or tribes as deemed under article 341 of the Indian Constitution" for the purpose of the constitution. Government of India act 1935, considered these scheduled caste population to be determined on the basis of following deprivation, particularly socio-economic; that they:

- Occupy low position in Hindu social structure
- Have inadequate representation in government services
- Are inadequately represented in the trade, commerce and industrial sector
- Suffer social and physical exclusion from the rest of community
- Lack educational development amongst the whole community.

Power Structure of Caste: A Social Perspective

The nomenclature of 'caste' is derived from the Portuguese word 'casta' 'which means 'breed' or 'lineage' or 'race'; known as 'jati' in Indian context that refers 'birth'. The structuralists define caste as a 'closed rank group' and cultural system viewed this as a 'set of values, believes and practices'.

According to Ketkar – "A caste as a social group having two characteristics:-

- First, membership is confined to those who are born of the members i.e., hereditary membership
- Secondly, members are forbidden by an inexorable social law i.e., endogamy."

According to C.H. Cooley – "When class becomes strictly hereditary, then it is a caste."

Caste as a form of social stratification that is associated with ritual status in hierarchical system of society, which is based on the concept of purity and pollution. According to Manuscript, the Brahman occupies uppermost rank followed by Kshatriyas, Vaishya and Shudras and untouchables stands even below the Shudras and made them to be discriminated with various disabilities as follow:

- Denial of access to public facilities i.e. roads, wells, courts, post offices, schools.
- Restriction of access to temples or where their presence was sought to pollute the higher class.
- Not allowed to learn Vedas and cannot become a holy man.
- Excluded from honorable and profitable occupation and therefore, restricted to do menial job.
- Remain outside the village due to residential segregation.
- Denial of using comforts and luxury goods and were denied to right to ride on horseback or bicycle, umbrella, gold, silver ornaments and palanquins to carry brides.
- Restrictions of access to services.
- Uses of different utensils were compulsory requirement
- Not allowed to do movement within prescribed distances of residences of higher caste.
- Imperatives of deference in forms of address, language, sitting and standing in the presence of higher castes. "Caste as an epitome of the Indian 'traditional' society, represent a 'closed system' in which generation after generation opt for similar kinds of work" that is in

contrast of the modern Western industrial societies as 'open system' of the social stratification, where individuals can opt for their occupation according to their abilities and could move up in the hierarchy system of society. Such mobility was impossible in the caste system. It is different from class system. While caste is traditional, class has emerged with the process of secularization of occupation and industrialization.

Non - Dalits: Who they are

Two perception about non-Dalit community, are predominantly famous:

- First, the non-Dalit are the one which are Dwija-born (twice-born); the Brahmins, Kshatriyas, Vaishyas and Shudras.
- Second, racially different and historically outsiders - the Aryans.

This Aryan theory, invented by Friedrich Max Muller (1823-1900), considered Shudras, untouchables and tribal as the 'natives' - the original inhabitants of the land called 'Bharat', and the Dwija-born as outsiders.

Ambedkar on Caste

B.R. Ambedkar viewed the rigidity of the caste system as it is based on graded inequality that is inherited in society "as a fundamental principle beyond any kind of controversy. These four classes are not only different but also unequal in status in the hierarchical social system and does not recognize equal need, equal work or equal ability as the basis of distribution of reward for labor". It is founded on the prescribed graded occupation that is inherited from generation to generation. There is confinement of interaction of people in the Hindu social order to their respective classes that is reflected in the "restriction on inter-dining and inter-marriages between people of different classes. He says that Hindu social order is primarily based on the 'Varna' or class as the unit of society rather than an individual. There is no room for individual merit and no consideration of individual justice.

He decries the division of society into varnas as it has failed to uphold liberty, equality and fraternity - the three pillars of a free democratic social order. He adds – "the most extensive manifestation of this spirit of isolation and separation is that castes are divided into sub castes. So, what fraternity can there be in a social order based upon such sentiments?" He considered "Hindu social order as against the 'equalitarian temper' that do not allow equality of a circumstances, institutions and lifestyle to develop. There is absence of 'liberty of action' because the occupation and status of the individuals are all fixed on the basis of their birth in a particular family. He was of the opinion that Hindus believe in the law by which people are to be governed, already exist in the Vedas and no human being is empowered to bring about a change in the existing laws".

According to Ambedkar, "this subdivision of a society is quite natural. But the unnatural thing about these subdivisions is that they have lost the open-door character of the class system and have become the self-enclosed units called castes. The question now arises were they compelled to close their doors and become endogamous, or did they close themselves of their Accord? For this, Ambedkar answered some have closed their doors, others found it closed against them. The one is a psychological interpretation and other is mechanistic, but they are complementary".

Ambedkar recites Gabriel Tarde's laws of imitation in this context – "imitation flows from higher to lower. The intensity of imitation varies inversely in proportion to distance and distance is understood here in the context of sociological meaning. By criticizing the caste and its division of labor or stratification of occupations; Ambedkar was of the opinion that caste system does not permit the readjustment of employment and hence caste becomes a cause of much of the unemployment in the country. It is based on the dogma of predestination".

Furthermore, he questions the wisdom of socialists and suggest that "religion, social status and property are all sources of power and without bringing reform in social order, one cannot bring about the economic change. He also cautioned the socialists that the proletariat or the poor do not constitute a homogeneous category. Indeed, they are divided or categorized not only on their economic status but also on the basis of caste and creed. Therefore, they cannot unite themselves against those who tend to exploit them. Communities in a graded order in the Hindu religion makes it impossible to organize a common front against the caste system. Castes form a graded system of sovereignty, high and low which indicates the jealously inherited of their status and are feared about the general dissolution of caste. They have fear about if this dissolution would happen, some of them would lose more prestige and power than others. Hence, it is not possible to organize a mobilization of the Hindus".

He was of the opinion in his "Annihilation of caste" that caste is a notion; it is a state of the mind. It is essential to attack on the sacredness and divinity of the caste in order to abolish or annihilate the caste system. In other words, the real way to annihilate the caste system is "to destroy the belief in the sanctity of the Shastra". Thus, he emphasized on the need to formulate political laws in a constitutional way in order to dismantle the caste system to promote the wellbeing and to empower the vulnerable people owing lower status.

The constitutional approach towards Dalit empowerment

The approaches and intervention of government towards the uplifting scheduled caste are primarily based on the following two considerations:-

- First, to overcome the deprivation, that the backward castes have inherited due to historical exclusion and, to possible extent, to bring them at par with others in the society.
- Finally, encouraging their effective participation in the social, economic and political processes of the country by providing them protection against exclusion and discrimination in the society.

In order to achieve these ends, government institutions needed a two-fold strategy consists of:

- Anti-discriminatory or protective measures;
- Development and empowering measures through their participation in the decision-making process of the

country.

Therefore, the educational development of these vulnerable castes is thrust area for the government as these communities have a "low literacy rate; high dropout rate at the primary, secondary and higher qualification level; low quality education and the existence of highly discriminatory and exclusionary practices, which are deterrent to their participation in the participatory empowerment". Therefore, the government entails:

- Improved qualitatively the educational infrastructure, especially in those areas inhabited predominantly with these backward castes;
- to ensure implementation of reservation system in educational institutions;
- providing financial support in terms of scholarships and fellowships at local, regional, national and international level;
- providing coaching facilities to these vulnerable social groups to build their qualitative capability;
- providing special hostels for the boys and girls;
- promote equal opportunities to these vulnerable social groups by ensuring and emphasizing particularly on girl/women education.

The safeguards have been provided in Indian Constitution to facilitate the implementation of the directive principles contained in Article 46 "The state shall promote with special care the educational and economic interests of the weaker sections of the people and in particular, of the scheduled castes and the scheduled tribes, and shall protect them from all social injustice and all forms of exploitation." For this purpose, various provisions related to SCs are contained in part 3 (fundamental rights); 4 (The Directive Principles of the state policy); 6,14,16, and 19 (appointment of ministers for the welfare of the SCs) of the Constitution. The Constitution of India guarantees-

- Article 14 – Equality before law
- Article 15 (4) – Advancement of any socially and educationally backward class or for SCs
- Article 16 (4) – Empowers the state to make provisions for reservation in appointments or posts in favor of any backward castes as citizens.
- Article 17 – Untouchability stands abolished and its practices in any form is forbidden.
- Article 46 – Promote, with special care, the educational and economic interests of the weaker sections of society and promises to protect them from social injustice and all forms of exploitation.
- Article 330 – Reservation of seats for SCs in democratic institutions and article 335 in the services, is a measure of positive discrimination.
- Article 340 – Empowers the state to appoint a commission to investigate the conditions of the socially and educationally backward classes; and
- Article 341 (2) – Specify the castes to be deemed as SCs.

The reservation policy plays an important role in the government services, state-run and state-supported "educational institutions, and various democratic political bodies; is part of the anti-discriminatory or protective measures". This is to ensure proportional participation of backward castes in public sector as well as in various political democratic bodies and institutions. This proportional participation of backward castes might not have been realized without this "positive discrimination" or "affirmative action" due to the prevalence of historical existing discrimination and exclusion. Thus, reservation policy is to ensure social justice to the disadvantaged groups by providing:-

* Safeguards for public employment/services,
* Provisions regarding entry into government educational institution,
* Provision related to reservation of seats in Central and state legislation in political bodies and institutions.

Conclusion

Notwithstanding the pan-character of the structure of caste, it varies from regions to regions due to having the different structures in different societies with different specifications. They vary from one caste structure to another caste structure even ideologically. Their understanding regarding the participation in the political institutions and structures are not identical for everyone and hence, caste is not a rigid or unidirectional unit, after all, instead it is of a dynamic identity. Sudipta Kaviraj argued, that "instead of crumbling with historical embarrassment, caste group, in fact, adapted themselves well to the demands of the parliamentary politics and in this sense, it created a democracy of castes in place of a hierarchy". Hence, we can say that caste represents the core of India in the power structure, and this is not only such institutions which give characteristics of the structure of social stratification. Instead, it is both an institution as well as an ideology. When we see this institutionally, then caste provides a definition for managing and organizing the socially organized groups in terms of their status in the socio-economic-politico milieu. On the other hand, when it is looked from the lenses of an ideology, then caste becomes a system of beliefs that provide legitimacy and reinforcing the prevailing framework of social inequality and discrimination. However, the transformation and alteration of existing realities of caste has led many possibilities for dynamic relationship between caste and the democratic political processes. Ergo, political scientists, with the coming up of 1960s, began talking about caste and politics in a different way. The eventual process of the institutionalization of Democratic politics has altered the caste equations from the so-called 'traditionally pure upper castes' to the 'middle level dominant castes' and thus, established a process of 'different power structure of caste in India'.

Class in Indian Politics

Introduction

Society naturally consists of different social groups and so there has been not a moment in history of human kind when different classes did not constitute the socio-political reality of Indian society. Classes are distinguished on various accounts like economic, social, and cultural or on other ethnic lines. The source of friction in society comes from any of these distinguishing factors and thus evolves a struggle among the class groups to prove their supremacy over others or challenging subordination by others and this shapes the power structure in society. In this chapter, we shall make an attempt to discuss the concept of class, theories on class and important scholarly viewpoints on class. We then will move on to discuss the history of class and class structure in India and lastly, we shall discuss class in relation to caste, both caste and class are important factors influencing power structure in Indian socio-political context.

Class as a Concept

An attempt to understand and define class must recognize that classes do not occur in vacuum rather they are a result of social and political dynamics influenced by historical churn of events or are influenced by certain contexts. A simple understanding of the term class can be drawn by an economic account where class relates to a system of social stratification or hierarchy drawn on economic lines like upper class, middle class or lower class. However, such a class configuration also has differences within these classes, making it a highly heterogeneous category. Class has come to occupy a key place in works of scholars. It has been defined differently by different scholars. Some of these definitions are stated below:

Ogburn and Nimkoff define class by stating that "the fundamental attribute of a social class is associated with social position of relative superiority and inferiority to other social classes".

MacIver and Page have said, "A social class is a portion of community marked off from the rest by social status. It is the sense of status, sustained by economic, political or ecclesiastical power, and by the distinctive modes of life and cultural expressions corresponding to them, that draws class apart from class, gives cohesion to each class and stratifies the whole society."

Ginsberg says, "A social class is any portion of community marked off from the rest by social status".

Gerth and Mills refer to term class as related to a group of people found in same situation.

John Harris writes that the concept of class "whether derived from Marx or from Weber, refers to the significance of economic endowments — whether material means of production or possession of particular skills ('human capital'), or cultural traits (referred to as 'symbolic capital'), or social connections (sometimes described as 'social capital'), which influence person's power in the markets vis a vis labor or money".

Class has come to occupy a key area of interest while understanding the structure of society and the dynamics of power involved therein, in space and time continuum, determining the class itself and its nature as well.

Class Structure in India

Class Structure in India is a highly variable. It is associated with the formation of class in India i.e. class formation which is influenced largely by factors like historical events and changes, the caste factor and the mobilization of class interests. Most importantly, in a country like India the analysis of class essentially requires an understanding of the cultural context of class which relates to the historical tracing of habits, behavior, thoughts and actions of a particular group of people and also class becomes more complex when seen with 93 respect to intersectional ties of class, party and status—the key aspects as highlighted by Weber. The Indian society can be broadly categorized into three broad class structures and it must be noted that class structures is deeply variant in India.

The Agrarian Class

India is dominantly an agrarian society and has since historical times reflected characteristics of class differentiation. Daniel Thorner, an American-born economist in his book—The Agrarian prospect in India outlined the model of agrarian class structure in India as highlighted below:

I. Maliks or Landowners: The Maliks were those who received their income from the land and kept high levels of rent and wage level was sharply low. The rent was paid by peasants, sharecroppers and sub-tenants. This section basically included big landlords and rich landowners.

II. Kisans and Rich peasants: This was the section which included working peasants who had property affiliations however the actual rights whether legal or customary is associated with landlords.

III. Mazdoors or Agrarian Laborers constituted the third category that derived and earned their livelihood primarily by working on land or plots. This includes poor tenants who lacked security as they had no access to tenancy rights and earned very less income. Sharecroppers also fall in this category who cultivated land on sharecrop basis and had lease of the land but without any security.

Lastly, the landless laborers were the ones who worked on land for wages.

The land reform policies and abolition of zamindari system in dependent India actually benefited largely the rich peasants. In decades of 1960s the Indian agriculture came to realize the panacea of high yielding variety seeds as part of Green Revolution which was implemented in states like Punjab, Haryana and Uttar Pradesh. This led to creation of class differentiation of rich and poor farmers rather say class polarization was evident and agrarian conflict took its hold in India's countryside.

John Harriss in his essay on Class underlines key changes in rural society with three main propositions:

(I) there is significantly less differentiation and polarization of peasant classes than it was in 1970s.

(II) The Land no longer is the most important deciding factor of status and power and it has also to an extent failed to set livelihood limitations on the poor particularly in wake of the surge in non-agricultural employment in nearby and also in distant areas. Also, as profit accruing from agriculture has declined people and mostly the younger generations are choosing to opt out of agriculture.

(III) The poor is loosening the ties of dependence and so is exercising little leverage over political space where the poor constitutes numerous rural laborers and small peasant petty commodity producers. Also, there has been an increase in number of armed insurgency in rural society making it a great internal security challenge for the Indian state to overcome.

The agrarian class has always played a key role in exerting claims for favorable agrarian policies and concessions from the state. The farmers have remained a key section for electoral gains in eyes of the political class. In contemporary times, the rural to urban migration and the crisis of agricultural economy, however, is changing the rural landscape with people opting out from agriculture. This may result to an extent to make agrarian class a less dominant force politically.

The Working Class

The Indian working class emerged as a prominent political force since the nineteenth century when India was still battling against exploitative colonial rule. The working-class agitations in pre independence era involved numerous cases of mill strikes, strikes in factories, railways strike among others. Initially the Congress did not come out in full support of representing these issues taking place in corners of India however with rise of economic nationalism, drain of wealth theory and with greater clarity between colonialism and nationalism, the Congress party and Communist Party of India played important roles in mobilizing and channeling the angst of population against the alien rule. Vivek Chibber writes that in post independence era the organized working class was very effectively co-opted by Congress through formation of Indian National Trade Union Congress (INTUC) in opposition to the Communist supported All India Trade Union Congress. The common view prevalent was that the working class has been fragmented and so weak however it was countered by scholar E. Teitelbaum, where he suggested that the functioning unions have remained constant and are increasing in size and there was less fragmentation at level of the firm where the industrial company negotiates with one or two unions. However, it needs to be understood that the Indian society has witnessed significant changes in its political economic sphere and thus the level of industrial disputes remains high and failure of state to reform labor friendly policies results in strengthening of the labor unions. The large number of informal workers exerts larger pressure targeted towards the state rather than the industrial sectors or the employers, as pointed out by Agarwal, further the demands are specifically for welfare benefits rather than worker rights. Agarwal also writes that informal workers "struggling not against informality but for rights within this status." It invokes the spirit of rights of women, right to livelihood, and housing among other crucial welfare benefits. Such a mobilization infuses a unique character to larger framework of democracy as these movements take form of social movement unionism as highlighted by P. Waterman (1993).

The Capitalist Class

This class includes the capital or the big business class. Rudolph and Rudolph stated that in India the business class interests are better represented than the interests of organized labor. Vivek Chibber analyzed the relationship of the Indian state and the business class where the Indian state failed to an extent in disciplining the big business class and the Indian state was ambiguous to the private-sector development. It was only with the change in political mood and attitude of the political class that the investment started to pour in and the business class responded to it positively. Also there have been efforts from both the sides — the Indian state and the business class to come to a point of consensus and the institutions like FICCI, ASSOCHAM, CII have helped to locate the meeting grounds in case of diverging goals of balancing growth and equity while achieving new heights of development.

The Middle Classes

The middle classes have an important role to play in country's politics as it takes a form of a continuum between the big bourgeoisie and the middle class. The middle classes constitute variant group in society mainly comprising the petite bourgeoisie who own small capital. It was Michael Kalecki who used the 'intermediate classes' term for referring to a class of small landowners, rich and middle peasants, merchants of rural and semi-rural township, small scale manufacturers and also retailers. Barbara Harris White uses the concept of intermediate classes and terms it as the 'local capital' as this class takes leverage of cultural, co-operative and philanthropic and trade association factors rather than direct channels of political parties. The other category of the middle classes which is more dominant is 'the new middle class' in words of Fernandes and Heller. This is the class which constitutes people with advanced professional credentials or accumulated cultural capital occupying positions of recognized authority in various fields. (Fernandes and Heller 2006)

Deshpande describes this middle class as one which is "dependent on cultural capital including English speaking skills and practicing cosmopolitan behavior of upper castes and the fraction of the middle class which articulates the hegemony of the ruling bloc in Indian society of giving voice to and linking or connecting the relations between the ruling bloc and the rest of society." (Deshpande 2003)

Another section of the middle class is the subordinate middle class who are salaries employs, having education capital which aspire to and try emulating to the practices of the dominant section of society as highlighted by

Fernandes and Heller.

Deshpande characterizes this section as "the 'mass fraction' engaged in exemplary consumption of ideologies which are produced by the elite fraction, thus investing them with social legitimacy". (Deshpande 2003)

With the neo-liberal economy becoming a widespread phenomenon, the middle classes who have reaped benefits with growing economy and most importantly proliferation of the service sector, they are now playing dominant role in electoral politics of the country, as contemporary developments stand to record.

Class Caste Nexus

The Indian society presents a unique case of caste-class nexus as they cut across each other. Caste-class intersections sharpen our understanding about the various social, economic and political relations we observe around them. The caste-class nexus does make the picture complex yet help us to grasp a more comprehensive and broader outlook of the power structure in context of India. Class plays out with caste as observed the dominant castes acquire more respect and social acceptance than the lower castes. Gough used the concept of caste and class nexus to in her analysis of mode of production as is reflected there are significant interconnections between caste, class, kinship, family and marriages with the forces of productions and the production relations. Joan Mencher highlights that the caste system serves as effective system of economic exploitation of the lower castes and they in turn remain strangled into lower classes of the society.

There is a section of popular opinion which seeks to understand caste and class differently. D'souza used the rigidity-fluidity dimension of social stratification where it was implied that caste belongs to the rigid framework whereas the class represents fluidity. But it must be understood that both caste and class are actually inseparables and both have contributed to social formation and gave shape to power structure in India. The caste-class overlap was more significant at the time of the independence when there were largely three broad classes including the landowners the cultivators, and the landless. However there have been significant developments since then with the universal adult franchise granting political right to each individual thereby serving as a great weapon of political assertion, the green revolution made ramifications in rural agrarian society, the economic reforms of 1991 and the Other Backward Class reservations have played huge role in changing the dynamics of caste class overlap. However, if seen in a broader perspective, the upper castes largely constitute the upper classes and the lower castes still occupy lower class positions in the class structure and so the caste and class are interactional and not opposite to each other.

Conclusion

This chapter has highlighted the various theories of class which further help us understand the nuances of the concept of class. The chapter also explains the dynamics of the class structure in Indian by tracing the class structure and its formation historically—in pre independence and post independence period. Therefore, it can be summarized that class has played a dominant role in Indian politics as it functions as a power structure by stratifying the society and also mobilizing class interests, showcasing the struggle for power in society. It must also be recognized at the same time that class does not acts in vacuum rather it asserts itself more strongly when seen in relation to the dynamics of caste. It must be finally acknowledged that any comprehensive attempt of studying Indian politics cannot remain oblivious to the dynamics of the class.

Patriarchy in Indian Politics

India has been and continues to be a patriarchal society, with women's general subordination and disempowerment usually indicated by patriarchy. It is a form of social organization in which the father is the supreme authority in the male lineage of the family, clan or tribe and descent, with the children of the clan or tribe of the father. Negatively, patriarchy can be said to be a social system in which men hold power by cultural norms and practices that favor men and preserve women's opportunities. Aristotle called active men, women passive. For him, "mutilated man" was a female, someone who has no soul. Throughout his opinion, women's biological inferiority often renders them inferior throughout her intelligence, her ability to reason, and hence her ability to make decisions. Since men are superior and women are deficient, men are born to rule and women are to be ruled. Patriarchy can be viewed and understood in many respects. If men hear the word 'patriarchy,' most of men will be on the defensive; and with its mention, most women will feel oppressed and dominated. As Allan B. Jonson states, "force and violence are promoted in a patriarchal society; it is because women are regarded as attractive and valid objects of male domination, and because in a society structured around authority, coercion and violent labor." In fact, power, supremacy, hierarchy and rivalry define the patriarchal system. According to him, patriarchy is "a type of society that is more than a set of men and women and cannot be understood simply by observing them." Therefore, patriarchy is a kind of society structured around certain types of social ties and ideas. Paradoxically, both our engagement affects our lives and gives us the chance to be part of changing or perpetuating it. Patriarchy is an issue that is complex. It is not just its character, male-dominated, male-identified and male-centered. There's a lot more to it than this and the link between its various parts. There is a collection of symbols and concepts at its heart patriarchy that constitute a society represented by everything from the substance of everyday conversation to literature and film. Patriarchal culture involves ideas about the nature of things, like men, women and society, with manhood and masculinity more closely associated with being male and womanhood and femininity relegated to the "other" marginal role. It's about how social life is and how it should be; about what people are expected of and how they behave. It's about feminine beauty standards, and masculine resilience, feminine vulnerability images, and male defense. The notion that women are weak and men are strong is believed by the patriarchy. In patriarchal societies, if they do not confine themselves to their positions, both men and women are ridiculed. In pre-patriarchal times, the experience, intelligence and virginity of a woman was respected and positively treated against the negative treatment and impotence associated with women in the present patriarchal times. Abeda Sultana says in her article, "Patriarchy conducts those social customs, rituals and social roles through socialization mechanisms to keep women under the rule of men. Patriarchy developed 'masculine' and 'feminine' characteristics to maintain male supremacy, private-public spheres through the cycle of gendered socialization. Socialization is considered to occur mainly during childhood, when boys and girls learn the right behavior for their specific gender. The foundations of a patriarchal system and culture are all agents of socialization structures such as family, faith, legal system, economic system and political system, educational institutions and media. Walby's patriarchal ideas clearly speak to patriarchy's private and public spheres. Whereas private patriarchy is practiced at home on the basis of materialism; where a woman has no power because she does not earn money in the form of services and emotional support despite the work and her contribution to the household. Public patriarchy is practiced at workplace and state. More often than not, the patriarchal system poses obstacles to the growth and development of women in their professions, in society and in personal life. Patriarchy is dividing women without their legal rights. Patriarchy is a system whereby in a number of ways women are kept subordinate. The subordination they experience on a daily basis, regardless of the class to which they belong, takes different forms – bigotry, disrespect, provocation, power, abuse, injustice, aggression – within the family, at the workplace and in society. Marxist feminists have tried to investigate not only 'patriarchy' but the association between patriarchy and the capitalist method of production. This is because they do not accept that women's subordination can be isolated completely from the other forms of exploitation and inequality that occur in capitalist societies. Like, class exploitation and racism; but they deny the ways in which orthodox marxism and socialist organizations have historically and literally exploited women and treated women's oppression as merely a side effect of class exploitation. Generally speaking, authority power lies in the male's hands in family, culture and state. In a society where men consider themselves superior to their female counterparts, women find it difficult to educate themselves; their families give priority to male child education, particularly in developing societies where resources are scarce and government is unable to provide all children with good quality free education. The male and the female child are classified differently, with preference for the male child. Most household women so unknowingly accept the patriarchy system that they themselves promote the system in their own households. In the second half of the twentieth century, feminist ideas modified and widened the definition of Patriarchy. In fact, precisely because it was considered only to apply to and characterize ancient civilizations, the social sciences had left it behind. But for many feminists, patriarchy is much more than empires that existed in the ancient past and goes beyond "the unequal distribution of power in certain areas of our society between men and women," as many dictionaries often describe it. Most forms of feminism, on the contrary, characterize Patriarchy as an unjust social system that subordinates, discriminates or oppresses women today. As Carole Pateman writes, "The political difference between freedom and subjection is the patriarchal construction of the difference between masculinity and femininity." The Patriarchy definition encompasses all the socio-political structures which is called Patriarchal Institutions that perpetuate and assert male dominance over women. Patriarchy is usually defined by feminist theory as a social construction that can be resolved by disclosing and critically analyzing its manifestations and institutions. Combining all these elements of Patriarchy, it can be described as: It refers to a historical process by "gradual institutionalization", which shows that Patriarchy is not universal, has not always existed, and is not equivalent in all cultures and generations. This, in effect, means that while men have power over women in all institutions that are considered important in every society, it does not mean that women have no power or rights, influence or wealth, nor does it mean that all women have or practice the same power. Therefore, as the Patriarchy becomes more complex, more women from specific groups are allowed access to certain institutions, even though they are almost never the most powerful people in those institutions. Through "sex-based political relationships" which mean, as Kate Millet explained so well, that Patriarchy accepted sexual and other relationships between the two sexes are political relationships through which men dominate women. By "Consensus on Women's Lesser Quality", It refer to a tacit and implicit consensus between each community member that women and everything related to women are worth less than men and everything related to men. We see this mirrored in the Sexist Language Institution, which defines the feminine as "the other," the male as the standard and the feminine as reflecting or containing the feminine. Through "consensus," which often refer to an ideology and its language usage that directly devalues women through assigning less importance and/or power to them, their roles, their jobs, their goods and their social environment than to men. By "patriarchal institutions", which refer to the collection of processes, traditions, values, theories and relationships that coordinate relatively stable patterns of human activity in terms of resource distribution, individual reproduction and the type of social structures within a given patriarchy. Such institutions are closely linked, developing, sustaining and transferring injustice from generation to generation. Many sociologists consider social structures such as states, families, human languages, universities, hospitals, businesses and legal systems as institutions. The "appropriation of the reproductive power of women" and the influence over their bodies and sexuality is the result of radical feminism. For instance, Shulamith Firestone explains how human reproduction, which happens in women's bodies, is legally manipulated and controlled by men and is used to benefit men or to keep women at men's mercy.

Origin of the Institution of Patriarchy

It is assumed that patriarchy originated from the male - female biological differences. In particular, women's biological advantages in bringing children created unequal social roles and assigned them duties such as motherhood, parenting, teaching and raising children by becoming fully dedicated to families. For women, "anatomy is destiny," to quote Sigmund Freud, and it is the biology of women that determines their psychology, productive ability and roles. In the same vein, Heywood suggests that men and women's social differentiation basically emerges from their biological distinction. Patriarchy is a problem for feminism. They argue that the biological difference in their positions can contribute to some discrepancy, but the former should not become the foundation of a sexual hierarchy in which men are dominant. The feminists are arguing patriarchy is man-made and the socio-economic and political structures of society have evolved historically. The interpretation indicates that colonization and expansion ventures have reinforced the patriarchy. People were deemed suitable for rugged journeys and harsh fighting conditions. In order to defeat enemies and extend their territories, their physical prowess was best remembered. Therefore, men were asked to come out and women were asked women to nurture their children. In addition, dependence for livelihood on agriculture and hunting required male labor. The male became the "bread winners" and the caretakers were the women. Gender-based social cleavages promoted patriarchy. All the differentiations, however, emanate from the biological differences and variations in women's psychological make-up to be compassionate and loving.

Features arising out of the practice of Patriarchy

Therefore, the above discussions clearly indicate that a patriarchal society is dominated by men, defined by men and based by men. Women's inequality and subordination is fundamental to the concept of patriarchy. The main characteristics that arise from patriarchy experience can be discussed as follows:

1. Patriarchy generate public private dichotomy–It simply implies that the private realm should be women's operating area and men should decorate the public realm.

2. Patriarchy encourages patrilineage and patrilocality–The ancestry line goes from father to son named patrilineage. In addition, the patriarchal order is patrilocal where the wife and off springs remain at the home of the parent.

3. Patriarchy entails patriarchal influence over the sexuality of women–Men decide women's dress code. Women are denied chores that require versatility in body movements and their effectiveness is derecognized and their employability is limited in non-conventional occupations. The women who run devices or riding vehicles are filled with animosity. Women are treated as the rituals, practices and cultural treasurers. Cultures highly value and encourage their involvement as devdasis, fasting practice. She is produced in securities and she becomes dependent on the patriarch.

4. Patriarchy controls the fertility of women–Women are treated by men as machines who produce children. Customary practices include male child preference and encourage female feticide, female infanticide and girl child negligence. The wishes and decisions of a woman are rarely respected in terms of the time of conception, the frequency of conception and the number of children that the family wishes to have. Her fertility is at the direction of man.

5. Patriarchy controls the labor of women–Patriarchy demands a male order, male supremacy and division of labor based on gender. Men rationalize leading, manipulating and yielding roles while women are given subordinate, executing and non-paying positions. The labor market favors men as opposed to women. Females are replaced by unpaid labour-power. Therefore, patriarchy gives centrality to men by relegating command and control to men and subordinate positions in all aspects of life to women.

Marriage and Patriarchy

It is important to get married as soon as possible so that she can go and settle in the house of her husband and take care of her in laws. Sometimes, even if, due to lack of family support, the woman wants to study and pursue a career, unfortunately she has to give it up for her parents or husband's sake. After marriage, the family name of the wife will be changed to that of her husband, or the husband's family name will be added to the wife's name, while the husband's name will remain the same. Likewise, their father's family name is given to children.

Often her own desires and needs are sacrifices. When, in keeping with the patriarchal social system, a woman goes forward and neglects what she is expected to do, she is blamed and sometimes not recognized as a good woman. On the other side, the man was able to do whatever he wanted. A woman may be lucky to find a husband who is loving and caring. If not, at the hands of her partner, she is a survivor of physical, mental or sexual violence. According to research carried out by the television series 'Satyamev Jayte,' which highlighted some very significant evils, issues and processes in Indian society, at least 70 percent of women in India are subject to domestic violence. It is not only for poor or uneducated families; it happens in every part of Indian society regardless of class and caste.

At home, under the patriarchal system, the word of the man is the last word in most households. Women are often regarded as stupid, unaware of what is happening in the world. The man is therefore in charge. The woman is there to take care of everybody's needs without ever having to feel as much as her household men as a human being. The man can taunt her whenever he likes; he can tell her off and treat her in the way he wants because she is his property.

When there is a divorce, the wife is often blamed for being unable to adapt, and her mother for being unconsidered about her children's so-called 'healthy' upbringing.

A woman is rarely paid equally at the workplace and is often not given equal opportunities for growth. On the workplace, there is sexual harassment; and it is considered better to remain quiet and not complain about it considering the patriarchal system, where men have the right to even abuse women sexually. In marriage, physical relationships are not considered rape in our country without the permission of a woman. Does that mean her husband's a married woman is a slave? She can't just say 'no' because she's a woman. Women feel uncomfortable going out alone at night in most countries, whether developed, emerging or underdeveloped. What's the reason? Because the male species, under the patriarchal social order, sees itself as a 'king' and a woman as a subordinate, an object of its desire, which he is unable to control, because that is not essential. It's the women who have to protect themselves or their men, their owners have to take care of them and protect them if they don't want harm to come their way.

Jonson distinguishes a person from a structure by providing detailed descriptions of a company and the game of monopoly. When a person joins a business or operates in that company, he/she acts in the manner anticipated in that company. Nevertheless, the person may not actually act in a corporate environment as he/she does; and behave entirely differently outside the workplace. Likewise, when he/she plays a monopoly game, he/she behaves in accordance with the rules of the game, making him/her a greedy person. In real life, the same person may not be a covetous selfish being.

We co-exist with the patriarchy. The behavior determines the social system and the behavior is determined by patriarchy. Patriarchy is dynamic; as we observe different regions, cultures, communities and groups, it subtly changes its shape and color. Patriarchy is also continuously being transformed and re-formed. We should change some rules as individuals; and change the social order for good and prevent ourselves from behaving like 'men' or 'women' and make our society less hierarchical, less aggressive and more respectful. Some find that there has been always patriarchy and that it is a way to maintain order in a society.

There is another school of thought, on the contrary, according to which patriarchy is manmade and can be modified. Hierarchy has been established through historical processes; it has not always existed. Patriarchy and monogamy evolved with the idea of private property as a historical process, according to Frederick Engels. According to Lerner, patriarchy was not an occurrence but a mechanism that evolved over a span of nearly 2500 years (from about 3100 BC to 600 BC) and a number of factors and forces responsible for establishing male supremacy as we see it today.

Patrilocal residence refers to the woman's travel to her husband's house after marriage. Because of this, there is no interest for the girl in her room. She is treated as a burden to be sent away to the house of her husband. When they grow older, the only son will take care of the parents. The moment the woman goes to the house of her husband, she becomes a burden and the husband's wealth. She relies on her husband economically. There is no interest in her contribution to the household. From birth to death, this subordination undermines the self-respect, self-confidence and self-esteem of girls/women and restricts their ambitions. Even the state does not support women in most cases of female subordination and does not deal with them, except in exceptional cases. In India and the political support that women enjoy is a farce, at least on paper. Which women need in terms of equal treatment, not reservations, but equal opportunities both domestically and socially? It is imperative that men and households be sensitized and made aware of the fact that their girls are human and have as much right to life and happiness as the boys.

Mahi Pal wrote an article 'Caste & Patriarchy in Panchayats.' We're going to take a look in this region through his article. Panchayati Raj has become a self-government institution in India. Reservation was made both for women and lower castes. Both the government of the state and the government of the union made a serious effort to elevate and treat women equally. To make this attempt, they called meetings and organized workshops. The government of Haryana invited women in power at the level of Panchayati Raj to attend a workshop to discuss their problems and challenges in the process of effectively performing their duties. At the local level, these women in power had many issues. Surprisingly, not one of them said about women, their safety, female rights and domestic violence. These women were unaware of schemes related to the development of women, children and dalits. Some of the women sarpanches faced issues from the upper caste and upper-class men; these sarpanches failed to fulfill their duties and to carry out development work in their areas, mostly because they were women.

Feminism in a world of Patriarchy

Feminism is the idea that women should be equal to men's political, financial, cultural, intellectual and economic rights. This involves different campaigns, ideas and ideologies, dealing with gender inequality concerns, promoting women's equality and advocating rights of women and interests. The history of feminism may be split into three waves, according to Maggie Humm and Rebecca Walker. The first wave was in the nineteenth and early twentieth centuries, the second was in the sixties and seventies and the third stretches from the nineties to the present.

"First-wave feminism refers to a phase of nineteenth and early twentieth-century feminist activism. It centered on de jure (officially mandated) inequality, primarily women's suffrage (the right to vote)". Feminists battled for the first wave thus: civil rights and political rights. This included legal rights relating to education and citizenship, among other issues. As a result, this opportunity was exploited by many western societies and women could climb up the social ladder a little higher. Finally, the human race would embrace the fact that women were also human beings who were supposed to have the same rights as men. First-wave feminism is a social phenomenon much more significant than normal. The great feminist movement has changed the course of history. Though, this did not contribute to the abolition of all forms of inequality, which it tried to eradicate, patriarchy shifted in nature, turning some of the hardwon changes into new women's traps. Some of these pitfalls came to life with the second wave of feminism, advocating for the expanded freedom of the sexual expression of women. Nowadays, this freedom of expression has contributed to the fact that pornography has been encouraged and some might argue that it has led to a new kind of subordination to the above-mentioned "public arena sexualization."

The Feminist Movement's "second-wave" refers to an era of feminist activism that began in the early 1960s and continued in the late 1970s. While first-wave feminism focused primarily on addressing legal barriers to equality, second-wave feminism tackled a wide variety of issues, including unofficial inequalities, official legal inequalities, sexuality, family, job and reproductive rights. The second wave of feminism came out with the saying, "Personal is political." In all battlefields, women fought for equal rights. We found out that there was no movement on equal rights. Women asked to be judged in and out of the home for their true value. By the early 1980s, when patriarchal sex-based laws were gradually repealed, it was considered that women had achieved their targets and succeeded in changing social attitudes about gender roles. It's right that there were legal changes, but perchance the social changes were not as significant as they might be. Feminism with the aid of gender studies has demonstrated that we play our gender roles in society where men are supposed to behave like men and women like women. Feminist scholars have created all sorts of powerful principles in an effort to explain and battle women's subordination with the priceless support of women's studies that later developed into gender studies. One of these ideas is essentialism, which is the kind of philosophy that encourages men to behave as men and women as women, as well as telling us that men and women are total opposites and placing this disparity on our innate nature. Since traditionally throughout history, this essentialism has infected many of us, characteristics such as power and aggressiveness have been linked to men, while at the same time women are expected to be sweet and passive in some cases. This ideology has brought us books such as: "Men are from Mars, Women are from Venus," written in 1992 by John Gray. Feminist writers have pointed to the bad influence of essentialism by noting that not all men and women are the same. In fact, "the duality that characterizes the Western way of thinking divides the world into distinctions such as man-woman, culture-nature and individual-society.

But feminists have pointed out that the state of society is being overly simplified. Where, for example, do hermaphrodites fit in this dualism? Sex/gender binary are another key concept of feminist thinking. Feminists described the difference between sex and gender in this way: sex refers to biological sex, but gender is used to define the cultural meaning that society gives to biological sex, that is to say, the perceptions that we have about masculinity and femininity. In fact, these requirements limit our freedom of action because all those who do not comply are at risk of persecution or even socially cut off from society. In formulating these concepts and many more, feminists have tried to influence the thoughts of society of people by showing us how since antiquity the patriarchy has dictated our thoughts and actions.

Feminism and subsequent studies on sex and gender have certainly been a great help in the battle of women for equal rights. As a result, this world's once-vast divide between the two sexes is shrinking with time and effort. Nowadays, as most people know, women have ascended the social ladder to unprecedented heights, leading some of them to become no less than prime ministers, cabinet ministers and other influential positions have fallen into their capable hands. Despite this; it's hard to describe the third wave of feminism because we're in the midst of it ... the third wave is about globalization, the sexualization of the public space and the new field of studies called 'gender studies' many feminists now struggle so that women can be seen as something other than sexual beings and accessories. The sexual freedom that some of us desired for women has become a major issue in today's world, and the mainstreaming of pornography, as described before, has only taken women's abuse to an increasingly dangerous level. This development has become very alarming, where very young or vulnerable women are often exploited through prostitution, sex industry or women trafficking.

There are many different branches of feminism that cross the three waves to complicate things more. The first wave produced radical, marxist and revolutionary feminism, where liberalism movements battled on behalf of women for formal and legal rights, and the second two, which grew stronger with the second wave, explored how the economic situation in society represented the inferior position of women. The second wave saw the rise of radical feminism that blamed liberal feminists for closing their eyes to the fact that traditional gender equality did not actually represent real equality. In short, radical feminists blame the patriarchy for the inferior status of women in society, where the word 'politics' in their minds applies to power-structured relationships and structures, whereby one group of people is dominated by another, and in this context the abuse of men against women is seen as a significant reason for the dominance of men over women.

Since the state is seen as an 'instrument' of patriarchal dominance and it is assumed that its non-intervention is part of the patriarchal system's rationale. Third wave feminists have changed the landscape in recent years with their growing participation in research and scholarships that seem to have resulted in engaging in political organizations and issues. It has been argued that "postmodernism, along with post-structuralism, is the idiom of much of feminism in the 1990s," but "postmodernism rejects master narratives" and "the quest for the underlying causes of inequality, exploitation, the revolution of history is removed from court."

The second wave is selecting a conservative feminist's point of view when there are new points of view. This might be because the personal is political as a second wave feminist. Although there have certainly been many significant changes towards may women's equality, I do agree that many events occurring in our homes, privacy and other issues that some would find private, should also be researched in more detail. For example: the physical and sexual abuse of women and children, pornography, prostitution, trafficking in human beings and finally the massive sexualization of the public arena that has undoubtedly had its devilish effects. The second wave was an advocacy movement, and I agree the constant review of society is dispensable if not accompanied by concrete action to improve.

Walby has clarified these standpoints rather extensively:

There are discrepancies between radical feminists on the basis of male supremacy, but this is often seen to include the exploitation of female sexuality and bodies, while male violence is seen as the root cause in some accounts. It is seen that sexual activity is built socially around male notions of desire, not female.

Furthermore, sexuality is seen as a major site of male domination over women, whereby men impose on women their notion of femininity. In contemporary society, heterosexuality is socially institutionalized and organizes many other aspects of gender relationships. In contrast to the conventional view that rape and battering are isolated instances triggered by psychological problems in a few people, male violence against women is considered to be part of a gender control system.

Feminist Challenge to Patriarchy

Patriarchy is a problem for feminists. I argue that the biological difference in their positions may contribute to some discrepancy, but the former should not become the foundation of a sexual hierarchy in which men are superior. The feminists are arguing patriarchy is man-made and the socio-economic and political structures of society have evolved traditionally.

Many feminist scholars conceptualize and examine patriarchy in various ways. We are contesting the hierarchy. We claim that the biological difference in their positions may result in some discrepancy, but the former should not become the foundation of a sexual hierarchy in which men are superior. Feminists challenge patriarchy as a tool to serve the males' interest. Patriarchal philosophy manifests itself to them in society's dominant awareness, culture, beliefs and practices. Feminists reject the use of the word "patriarchy" and prefer the term "gender oppression" to replace it. Michele Barret argues that we sometimes use the term patriarchy hedonistically to indicate its unchanged presence. But the feminist attempt to ensure gender equity will soon challenge the continuity of patriarchy with the current efforts to gender mainstreaming. Patriarchy is changing, although continuity of certain features is still being noted today.

Summary

Understanding patriarchy explains why women sometimes fight for their rights and sometimes just struggle to survive free of men's power and authority that threatens them. Women professionals have been dramatically successful in questioning patriarchal norms as being educationally, politically and socially as well as in terms of their abilities. Millennials have gained financial independence, more bargaining power within the family, and a sense of empowerment outside the society, strengthening their position in decision-making that their older generation never had. Even then, they see their duties to their husbands, children, friends, and other close relatives as the most important and continually prioritizing their families over their jobs. It can be concluded that although women have entered the public domain and become part of market forces, they remain consistent with their private sphere affiliation and related patriarchal standard obligations. Only from the understanding of their unequal state of being can a feminist perspective be built that allows men and women to liberate their minds from patriarchal thinking and traditions and eventually build a world free from domination and patriarchy, a world that is truly human.

CHAPTER V

Religion and Politics

Introduction

This chapter is about relationship between religion and politics. It discusses the nature of relationship between religion and the state, of religion with the community, individual and with democratic values such as liberty and equality, and with ethics.

Secularism

Secularism is one of the most crucial issues in the current political scenario in world. Yuval Noah Harari, the author of *21 Lessons for the 21st Century* includes secularism among 21 most urgent issues of the 21st century. In India too, secularism has been at the core of academic, popular and political discourse. Some questions are often raised about secularism: about its relationship with religion, state and other institutions, faith, religious communities, place of individual, democratic values such as freedom and equality about religion, and ethical values.

The central issue in secularism is religion. Secularism in a society implies that the religious supremacy of a community does not lead to discrimination and persecution of religious minorities. The meaning of secularism depending on the extent of relationship religion has with the attributes mentioned above, i.e, relationship with religion, state and other institutions, faith, religious communities, place of individual, democratic values such as freedom and equality about religion and ethical values.

There are three meanings of secularism according to different perspectives: one talks about relationship between the religion and the state; two, is about the possibility or impossibility of applicability of secularism in India; and the third is about equal respect to all religions or *sarva dharma sambhav*. These perspectives have been reflected in the debate within the Constituent Assembly, popular and academic discourse in India. As you will read in this unit, the debate on secularism in India, in the Constituent Assembly, and academic discourse has involved these three meanings to varying levels.

According to Rajiv Bhargav success of secularism depends on certain factors. These are democracy and independence of the state from pressure of classes and ethnic groups in society which again depends on presence of state. Democracy depends on pacification of politics, i.e. peaceful competition or competition without violence. In fact, secularism is associated with values which are linked with democracy and equal citizenship. Yuval Noah Harari underlines that in a secular society, people belonging to different faiths – Hindus, Christians, Muslims, and atheists follow certain ethical codes. These ethical codes are enshrined in the values or secular ideals such as truth, compassion, equality, freedom, courage, and responsibility. For secularists, truth is different from belief, and there is no single source as custodian of truth. Compassion implies a "deep appreciation of suffering", to reduce sufferings in the world in best possible way. Since sufferings are universal, the commitment to truth and compassion result in commitment to equality. The search for truth can be achieved with freedom to think, investigate, and experiment. Courage includes value to fight biases and oppressive regimes, to admit ignorance and "venture into unknown". Responsibility means to not rely on higher power to address problems facing societies, no divine power needs to be credited for it. The developments result from knowledge of human beings themselves and their compassion.

According to DE Smith, Secularism can prevail in a secular state. What is secular state? In DE Smith's model in *India as a Secular State*, a secular state can be identified by its dealing with three subjects: exclusion of state in relationship between individual and the religion (religious liberty); relations between individual and state in which religion is excluded (individual as citizen); and state neutrality. In Smith's perspective, India had prospects of success of democracy: characteristics of secularism are present in Hinduism. However, there have been challenges in consolidation of secular state in India: caste and community loyalties which could easily turn into communal rivalry and conflict. Gallenter finds Smith's critique of Indian secularism unconvincing: countering Smith, he contends that Indian state departs from principles of secularism by giving subsidies to religious schools and bodies, promoting Hinduism, and compromising its secular credentials. For him, precondition for a secular state to succeed lies in presupposing a normative conception of religion with capacity to judge and evaluate religion. In his opinion, the compromise in India on secularism, could be visible in the Constituent Assembly the debate on religious liberty (right to religious worship, religious practice, whether the state should recognise only linguistic minorities or linguistic minorities" as well); on citizenship (universal civil code, religion-based political reservation); and on state neutrality (whether the state should give instructions to the state aided schools).

Akil Bilgrami contests the notion of secularism as merely state's neutrality and equidistance from different religions. Bilgrami rejects this notion and provides an alternative notion. He argues secularism does not emerge in all historical contexts. It emerges in some historical contexts. It emerges where there is threat of "majoritarianism". It can also emerge in the contexts which are not fully modernist. Secularism is different from secular and secularisation. Secularism is a political doctrine. A person may remain secular simultaneously retaining his/ her religious identity.

Secularism in Indian Constitution

Indian Constitution did not include the word secularism when it commenced on January 26, 1950. Although secularism was not mentioned in the Constitution, the fact that Independent India became a democracy, secularism was implied in it as a cardinal principle, a fait accompli, not needing its mention. But it was incorporated in the Preamble of the Constitution by 42nd Constitutional Amendment in 1976. Later, the Supreme Court ruled in the Bhommai judgement that secularism is a basic feature of the Constitution. Besides, provisions in Articles 25-30 protecting the rights of religious minorities in the Constitution emerged from debate in the Constituent Assembly of India: these signify values of secularism. The questions whether word secularism should be included in Indian Constitution, what kind of secular state India needed to become ("a secular state in a religious country"), whether separation of state from religion was a testimony for secularism, whether a secular state was contingent on a secular society or whether state that respects all religions equally meant presence of secularism in India, were discussed on October 17, 1949. The opinions on these questions were divided in the Constituent Assembly. Finally, the assembly decided to not include the word secular in the Preamble. However, there was an agreement among all members of the Constituent Assembly to establish India as a secular state. And most of them agreed that separation of religion and state was related to democratisation of society.

Shefali Jha identifies three alternative arguments on secularism which were debated in the Constituent Assembly. She terms the first argument as "no concern theory of secularism". The proponents of this argument argued that religion should not be concern of the state. Religion is a private affair and there should be separation between religion as a private affair and the state (public affair). People have liberty to practice religion as a private affair. The state should recognise an individual as a citizen not as a person from a religion. The principal representative of this argument were K.T. Shah, Tajamul Husain and M. Masani. The second line of argument also suggested that religion and state should be separated. But their argument was just opposite to the first argument. While the first kind of argument contended religion was a personal matter for the state to intervene, this argument suggested that religion was a system of absolute truth. Association of religion would not weaken the state but would demean religion. Whims of the majorities which keep changing should not be allowed to have a say in a democratic state. The third theory which Shefali Jha describes as "Equal Respect Theory of Secularism" argues that since in India religion was the most important part of people's life, the state should respect all religions equally along with maintaining a distance from religions. The most vocal advocate of this argument was K.M. Munshi. He argued "we had to evolve a characteristically Indian Secularism". In his opinion, India can not have a state religion; nor can a rigid line be drawn between the religion and the state. In this view a people's state can not be founded on a kind of secularism that is contemptuous of religion. Since most religions preach tolerance, if the state allows public sphere to religion it would not lead to inter-sectarian strife. Jaya Prakash Narayan argued that it was not religion but use of religion for social, economic and political purposes that leads to communal violence.

The points in debate on secularism which were discussed in the Constituent Assembly and in the 1950s were discussed in the debate on the theme which occurred later. One such debate represented a term which came to be alluded to as "anti-secularism". Like an argument given in the Constituent Assembly, advocates of anti-secularism are not opposed to secularism per se. What they are opposed to is the notion of secularism which suggests separation between religion and the state. They are critical of both communal-fundamentalist (Hindutva) and secularists. According to the advocates of anti-secularism, since India is a religious society, religion and the state can not be separated. They consider the notion of separation of religion and the state a western notion, which is not applicable to a religious society like India. Roots of real secularism can be traced in Indian traditions, which have been tolerant. Secularism can be achieved by equal respect for all religions (*Sarva Dharma Sambhava*). The main advocates of anti-secularist perspective are Bhikhu Parekh, T.N. Madan and Ashis Nandi. Especially, Madan considers secularism as a "gift of Christianity" and Nandi has "an anti-secularist agenda" to critique secularism. According to Achin Vanaik, they focus on six general themes regarding Indian society: modernity, understanding of culture, civilisation, religion and Hinduism, past and present; secularism and secularisation; particularism and universalism, individualism and communitarianism; and neo Gandhianism. While they share common point that state should respect all religions equally and Indian tradition has been a tolerant tradition, they have differences.

Rajiv Bhargava argues that the notion of secularism needs to be reconceptualised or re-imagined. Instead of focusing on state-church relationship the following is needed: (i) secularism should be focused as a response to deep religious diversity; (ii) diversity must be understood as enmeshed in power relations; hidden potential of religion-related domination must be understood; (iii) the two moves can help us to view secularism as a response to institutionalised religion (inter-and intrareligious) domination: secularism is not against religion; and it is opposed to institutionalised religion-based domination; (iv) and, only by maintaining principles distance a secular state can show critical respect to all religions and philosophical world views. He explains Indian secularism in terms of the notion of principled distance. He states "the idea of principled distance entails a flexible approach to the issue of state's inclusion or exclusion of religions and to the issue of engagement with or disengagement from religion, which at the level of law and order depends on the context." He classifies secularism into two kinds: political and secular.

According to some scholars (Smith, Tambia), secularism in India is facing crisis. There are external and internal factors responsible for this. External factors include - breakdown of Congress, increasing centralisation of power of the state and secessionist movements in the 1980s - in Punjab and Kashmir and implementation of Mandal Commission Report. Internal factors include – totalising world-view of which secularism is a part (Madan and Nandi) and demand for equidistance which can not be met by any state (Chatterjee).

Secularism and Religious Groups

Secularism and secularisation are two inter-related concepts. But in the academic and political discourse, it is the former which has received more attention. Several articles published in *Economic and Political Weekly* (Vol. 58, No. 50 Dec. 14, 2013) discuss the notion of secularisation and its relationship with secularism and several related aspects with reference to India, Pakistan and Bangladesh. It is about the nature of relationship about rights of religious groups and individuals within them. It is also about ethics or morality.

Secularisation means absence of influence of religion on public policies and social relations. But it does not negate religion itself. It is about how religion is the basis of favour or discrimination. It is about modernisation and modernity.

Secularisation must be "collective normative project"; whereas secularism in Europe was not "launched as a programme of collective action" (Rajiv Bhargava). Using notion of secularisation, Joya Chatterjee explains how that following the partition, both India and Pakistan followed policy of secularisation, which was partial. Both got busy in addressing non-religious issues of partition affected families: rehabilitation of the refugees. However, the secularisation was partial. It was a limited secularisation which did not permeate lower parts of state machinery.

Secularism has broadly two meanings: one, separation of religion from the state; and two, equal respect to all religions by the state or *sarvadharmsambhav*. Originally, the Preamble of the Constitution did not mention the word secularism. It was inserted into the Preamble by the 42nd Constitutional Amendment. The Constituent Assembly discussed whether secularism should be mentioned in the Constitution. There were three broad arguments in the Constituent Assembly: One argument suggested that since religion was a personal affair, there was no need to discuss it; Second argument contended that there should be separation between religion and that state; and, the third argument stated that the state should respect all religions equally or there should be *sarva dharma sambhav*.

Secularism denotes relationship between religion, state, institutions, social groups and individual. There are two notions of it: One, suggests a distance between religion and the state or equal distance or request to all religions by the state; another, talks about the relationship of religion with communities and individuals about democratic values such as freedom and equality, and morality.

In the Constituent Assembly, there were three types of arguments on secularism: One, the state should not interfere in religious matter; two, state and religion should be separate because religion is higher than the state/ beyond the scope of the state; and three, the state should pay equal respect to all religions.

The anti-secularists argue that secularism which preaches distance between religion and state is western context. In a country like India where religion is an essential aspect of like, religion and state can not be delinked. The real secularism can be traced in Indian traditions, which is marked by tolerance. True secularism can be achieved by following the principle of *sarva dharma sambhav* (equal respect to all religions).

Secularism denotes distance between religion and the state or equal respect to all religions. Secularisation denotes absence of the impact of religion on the state policies about social groups. It is also about how moral or ethical values shape attitudes about followers of different religions.

The idea of principled distance is propounded by Rajeev Bhargava. It denotes a flexible approach to state's engagement or disengagements with religions and to their inclusion or exclusion by the state. The level of engagement, exclusion or inclusion depends on context, nature and current state of religions.

Communalism

Communalism is an ideology which shapes the vision of members of a community, formed on the basis of common religion, about themselves, other religious communities, nationalism and the state. In their book *India's Struggle for Freedom*, Bipan Chandra and others, underline that communal ideology consists of three elements. The first element underlines the belief that people from similar religious community have similar secular interests such as political, economic, social and cultural interests. The second element denotes that the people belonging to different religious communities do not have common secular interests – social, economic, cultural or political interest. The third element or phase of communalism shows a stage in which the relations between different religious communities are seen as mutually incompatible, hostile and antagonistic.

Communalism is linked to another concept, e.g. communal violence. Both are different but inter-related. Communalism is a consciousness and when this consciousness gets expressed in terms of violence between two different religious communities it is called communal violence. Different religious communities do not become communal own their own. Nor do their relations turn into communal violence automatically. Religious communities are turned into communal communities by certain sections of society and they can convert relations between such communities into communal riots. Such sections can be political leaders, activists, middle classes or community leaders. They explain to the members of their respective communities that the other community is responsible for their problems. In certain politically suitable situation or context they are able to mobilize their respective communities into communal violence.

There have been different approaches to the way communalism can be studied. First has been the approach which may be called empirical approach used by various scholars starting Ashgar Ali Engineer in which different communal riots were studied and general conclusion have been drawn. A large number of scholars such as Amrita Basu, Paul Brass, Asutosh Varshney etc. have followed this approach to test their theories.

The second approach has been Materialist approach. This approach underlines the need to study social and economic conditions, role and nature of the state and ideology to understand communalism. In this approach, the incidents of communal violence are studied as a reflection of these factors. K.T. Shah, Bipan Chandra, Achin Vanaik, C.P. Bhambhri, Aditya Mukherjee have followed this approach. The third approach has been the essentialist approach where the communities are already seen to be different and living across fault lines with separate identities. Huntington, the American political scientist in his very celebrated book *Clash of Civilizations* has presented an outline of such approach.

Origins of Communalism

Communalism as a belief or an ideology has been the product of the colonial rule in India. In this sense it is product of modern times in India. Earlier also, there were large number of instances of inter-sect or inter-cult or religious conflicts and violence. But they were not communal in the sense it came to be understood from the mid-nineteenth century. The communalism in India largely was product of the colonial policies towards different communities, especially after the 1857 mutiny. The challenges faced by the colonial rulers in the latter half of the nineteenth century became the reasons for them to devise policies that promoted communalism. Among these challenges included criticism of the colonial administration by a new intelligentsia, which had emerged in India by mid-nineteenth century. This intelligentsia, most often, was the product of the new English education. This intelligentsia began to realize that people of India were suffering due to the colonial rule. Transcending linguistic, caste sectarianism or cultic identities the new intelligentsia sought to generate national consciousness against the colonial administration. Thus, the new intelligentsia, trained in both traditional knowledge and the new western knowledge through English Medium wanted a Indian people emerge as nation. This consciousness led them to attempt to constitute a 'national community' consisting of Indians of different sections of society. This was to contest the colonial constructs of a society and polity.

The colonial authorities responded to the challenge of growing national consciousness being generated by the efforts of the new intelligentsia. They did so by the following strategies: debunking the notion that Indians who had multiple diversities could be united as a nation, by creating a colonial knowledge and by highlighting differences among people which existed on the basis of religion, caste, language, etc. and by introducing religion-based representation in the legislative/political bodies. As a part of such knowledge, James Mill wrote a book *The History of British India*, in which he argued that history of India can be divided on the basis of religion into three periods: ancient, medieval and modern. Mill argued that ancient period in India's history symbolized India's golden period when she was the ruled by the Hindus; in medieval period, the Muslim invaders destroyed the glorious ancient Indian history and established Muslim rule; and the modern period denoted the end of the Mughal rule and establishment of the British rule in India. Such periodization of Indian history has been used by the communal historians and the colonial authorities to divide the society on communal lines. As most of the intelligentsia came from the upper crust of the Hindu society, its growth and ideas could be shown to be detrimental to the interest of Muslims by the Muslim intelligentsia and traditional elite. In 1987, Dufferin (Viceroy) and A. Colvin, Lt-

Governor of UP attacked Congress for being anti-imperialism. Syed Ahmad joined the attack thinking that it would help in getting Muslim share in administrative and professional positions increased. He believed that with the growth of Hindu intelligentsia and middle classes, the dominance of Muslims declined. Solution to Muslims dominance lay in enabling Muslims to get English education. For this purpose, he founded Anglo Mohammedan Anglo Oriental College in 1875 which later became AMU (Aligarh Muslim University). Meanwhile, a new Muslim middle class too was emerging at that time. However, its late arrival witnessed an already entrenched Hindu middle class which by 1870s onwards was quite vocal and anti-colonial in its approach. One of the strategies of the traditional Muslim elite and new middle class was to demand that they should be given preferences of representation in public institutions. The demand for reservation in jobs and educational institutions by the middle class soon got converged with the demand of the Muslim elite for more political power via statutory reservations in the legislative and other bodies. This led to the formation of the Muslim League in 1906 which also saw the active prompting by the British colonial government. In other areas, for example, the British encouraged sections from among the Hindus too with such favours as they seemed to divide the emerging national unity under the Indian National Congress. The demand for reservation in government jobs and representation of legislative bodies to the Muslims resulted in similar demands from some sections of the Hindus. And a competition between some sections of Hindu and Muslim intelligentsia took place for reservation in government jobs and legislative bodies. Later, these demands views were voiced by Muslim League.

In fact, the earlier Muslim intelligentsia and later Muslim League represented sections of Muslim landlords and middle classes and their vision and demands were common.

For some historians, Hindus had all the glory which was destroyed by the Muslim invaders while the Muslim communal historians saw the British as destroyer of the glory of Islam. According to them the Islamic glory had to be restored once again. This could be done by establishing an Islamic rule. These two versions represented two-nation theory. The policy level intervention to divide the Indians on communal lines included introduction of separate electorate in 1909 (Morley Minto Reform). According to the policy of separate electorate, in 1909 municipal elections, Hindu and Muslims contested from separate constituencies, where candidates and the electorate belong to the same religion. Separate electorate was political manifestation of communal divide. From the 1920s, the demands for more representation in the councils etc. was needed to be widened and so was popular participation. The 1920s saw the emergence of Khilafat movement which for the first time brought many Muslim into the larger political fold. This meant that the seeds of separate identities based on non-religious interests but along with the religious lines planted. The colonial government however tried to fragment the movement by organizing the Round Table Conference in 1930-32 in which representative of all conceivable groups and sectional interests were invited.

In comparison to Hindus, the rise of Muslim educated in English was limited. Educated Hindus and Muslims competed for government jobs. It gave a feeling among some sections of the new elite/middle class from both communities that because of the other community, they were not getting jobs and representation in political institutions. The Hindus viewed that their interests were antagonistic to Muslims interests and vice-versa. As we know in communalism the secular interests of different religions communities are antagonistic. Thus, communalism in India grew between the late nineteenth century and the partition of the country.

Communalism and the State

Communalism often leads to communal violence between different religious communities. There are several examples of communal violence in India. Communal violence is also result of intermingling of religion and politics. In the post Independent India, communalism has become part of the competitive electoral politics. According to K.N. Pannikar (1990), politics and communalism have become complementary, reinforcing each other in the post Independence period. State can devise policies which can either stop or encourage communalism. It can also play partisan role in communal politics. The state can play an important role in the spread or prevention of communalism. The nature of state's role on communalism depends on the nature of pressure of social groups on it and composition of the personnel in the state institutions and political context. Thus, the state functions under the pressure of different social groups and classes. These also include religious communities. As you have read above, the colonial rule promoted religious divisions: the policy was based on preferential treatment and discrimination. According to C.P. Bhambri, the post-Independence India inherited the legacy of religious backwardness and religious conflict. The state in India is placed in paradoxical situation: on the one hand it has to act through rules and regulations, new technology; on the other hand, it has to deal with the society where symbols, rituals and inherited social regulatory mechanisms exist. Indian state faced the challenge of losing loyalty if it is perceived to be acting against traditional practices – Muslim personal law (1985), Operation Blue Star (1984), Sabrimala (2019). In democratic society such as India, the state functions under the pressure of different social forces. It becomes a site of multiple ideologies and tendencies – including secularists and communalists. In the post Independence period, the Indian state has followed the strategy for managing conflicts – of oppression and cooptation: it makes compromises with communalism and casteism. And the exploiting classes have exploited religious sentiments to legitimize exploitation in the society. Zoya Hasan (1990) argues that the state surrendered to the pressure of religious fundamentalist in Muslim Women's Bill and Ram Janma Bhumi case.

Communalism and Media

Media, in both its traditional and newer forms, helpe ideologies and ideas to spread. As has been discussed in the rise of public sphere by Jurgen Habermas in the context of Europe, the public associations, clubs, public gatherings and later on print media which included newspapers, novels, textbooks, etc. have all helped many ideas to spread. Benedict Anderson, for example, called nation as an *Imagined Community* as it was created because of spread of imagined ideas of nation by the print media since the 18th century onwards. In relation to communalism in India, the media plays an influential role in creation and spread of communalism. Its role becomes crucial in reporting, explaining and commenting on communal riots or violence; about the reasons for occurrence of communal violence, role of leaders of different communities and politicians. The media includes print media – newspapers, magazines, and electronic media (television channels) and social media (WhatsApp, face book, tweeter, email). While media plays a decisive role in generating awareness among the people, on several occasions it has contributed to the spread of communal divide in the country. In the recent past, fake news, have become quite frequent to arouse communal passion in the society. Many of the news in the media are based on rumours and unverified facts. The social media for example has a reach which very few previous media had. It is also not controlled through censorship and other ways; any news or information, which may cause violence or animosity among different groups of people travels rapidly.

Communalism is an ideology which preaches that communities are formed on religious lines. And members of a community share common interests which are incompatible with the interests of other religious communities. In certain political contexts, communalism can lead to communal violence. This happens because of the role of political or community leaders. Communal violence which the post-independent India has seen can be traced to the colonial period. Sometimes communalism gets expressed in the form of communal violence. This can happen when some sections of leaders or political activists convert relations between religious communities into conflict. In past few years social media have also become source of communal divide.

Communalism is an ideology which shares the visions of members a community formed on the basis of religion about themselves, other communities and nationalism. It has three elements: first, members of a religious community share common interests; two, people from two different religious communities do not share common interests; and three, relations between different religious communities are incompatible and hostile.

Communalism and communal violence are different but inter-related. The former is an ideology which preaches that people from a religious community share common social, economic, political and other kinds of interests which are incompatible with the interests of other communities. Communal violence is violent expression of the differences between different religious communities.

It emerged during the second half of the nineteenth century, the colonial period. It was product of the divide and rule policy of the British. The policy was reaction to critique of colonial policies by the newly emergent intelligentsia. The responded to the critique of colonial rule by encouraging the intelligentsia and middle classes to make demands for reservation in jobs and representation in political institution on religious lines. They introduced separate electorates through Morley-Minto reforms on 1909. Consequently, it resulted in genesis of communalism in India.

CHAPTER VI

Parties and Party Systems in India

Introduction

Political party may be termed as a combination of some people who organise themselves to work unitedly for the achievement of common objectives having similar opinion regarding public issues and problems of the country. In this regard it is noteworthy that such parties pursue their political ambitions. It is an organization of the citizens. While discussing about the origin of political party it is seen that it originated in England at first. During the reign of the Queen Elizabeth I, the Puritans actually made the good beginning of political party when they worked together unitedly in the Parliament.

The political parties may be classified into three main types depending upon the party's role and position in the formation of the government or administrative machinery – (a) One-party system or Single party system (b) Bi-party system or two party system and (c) multi-party system. In the first type the presence of only one party, in the second type two party and in the third type presence of more than two parties are supposed to exist.

In the above words, it has been said that the political parties are indispensable organs in modern democracy. This has been recognised in almost all the states (countries) of the world now a days, because almost all the states are being ruled in a democratic system. So, the political parties are said to have steered the administration of the country.

In modern time without political parties one cannot expect to govern the state. In a democracy, political parties

114

plays a very significant role. Generally democracy is a form of government "by the people, for the people and of the people." In other words, Democratic rule (administration) indirectly means as the rule by the political parties. In a Parliamentary Democracy, the political party getting majority forms the government to rule. Whereas in the Presidential form of government, the leader (the President) of the majority party rules and under the Communist rule, the communist party governs. Moreover, in all the countries, the political parties take the initiative in the moulding of the public opinion. Therefore, in the democratic government, the political parties control the country's administration and the other political activities. Thus there is the necessity of studying about political parties. Political Parties are easily one of the most visible institutions in a democracy. For most ordinary citizens, democracy is equal to political parties. If we travel to remote parts of the country and speak to the less educated citizens, we could come across people who may not know anything about our Constitution or about the nature of our government. But chances are that they would know something about our political parties. At the same time, this visibility does not mean popularity. Most people tend to be very critical of political parties. They tend to blame parties for all that is wrong with our democracy and our political life. Parties have become identified with social and political divisions.

Necessity of Political Parties

Basically, Political Parties fill political offices and exercise political power. Parties do so by performing a series of functions:

(a) Parties contest elections:- In most of the democracies, elections are fought mainly among the candidates put up by political parties. Parties select their candidates in different ways. In some countries, such as the USA, members and supporters of a party choose its candidates. Now more and more countries are following this method. In countries like India, top party leaders choose candidates for contesting elections.

(b) Parties put forward different policies and programmes and the voters choose from them:- Each of us may have different opinion and views on what policies are suitable for the society. But not government can handle such a large variety of views. In a democracy, a large number of similar opinions have to be grouped together to provide a direction in which policies can be formulated by the governments. This is what the parties do. A party reduces a vast multitude of opinions into a few basic positions which it supports. A government is expected to base its policies on the line taken by the ruling party.

(c) Parties play a decisive role in making laws for a country:- Formally, laws are debated and passed in the legislature. But since most of the members belong to a party, they go by the direction of the party leadership, irrespective of their personal opinions.

(d) Parties form and run governments:- As we noted last year, the big policy decisions are taken by political executive that comes from the political parties. Parties recruit leaders, train them and then make them ministers to run the government in the way they want.

(e) Role of opposition:- Those parties that lose in the elections play the role of opposition to the parties in power, by voicing different views and criticising government for its failures or wrong policies. Opposition parties also mobilise opposition to the government.

(f) Parties shape public opinion:- They raise and highlight issues. Parties have lakhs of members and activists spread all over the country. Many of the pressure groups are the extensions of political parties among different sections of the society. Parties sometimes also launch movements for the resolution of problems faced by people. Often opinions in the society crystallise on the lines parties take.

(g) Parties provide people access to government machinery and welfare schemes implemented by governments:- For an ordinary citizen it is easy to approach a local party leader than a government officer. That is why, they feel close to parties even when they do not fully trust them. Parties have to be responsive to people's needs and demands. Otherwise people can reject those parties in the next election.

This list of functions in a sense answers the questions asked above. We need Political Parties because they perform all these functions. But we still need to ask why modern democracies cannot exist without political parties. We can understand the necessity of Political Parties by imagining a situation without parties. Every candidate in the elections will be independent. So no one will be able to make any promises to the people about any major policy changes. The government may be formed, but its utility will remain ever uncertain. Elected representatives will be accountable to their constituency for what they do in the locality. But no one will be responsible for how the country will be run. We can also think about it by looking at the non-party based elections to the panchayat in many states. Although, the parties do not contest formally, it is generally noticed that the village gets split into more than one faction, each of which puts up a 'panel' of its candidates. This is exactly what the party does. That is the reason we find Political Parties in almost all the countries of the world, whether these countries are big or small, old or new, developed or developing. The rise of Political Parties is directly linked to the emergence of representative democracies. As we have seen, large societies need representative democracy. As societies became large and complex, they also needed some agency to gather different views on various issues and to present these to the government. They needed some ways, to bring various representatives together so that a responsible government could be formed. They needed a mechanism to support or restrain the government, make policies, justify or oppose them. Political Parties fulfill these needs that every representative government has. We can say that parties are a necessary condition for a democracy.

Main Political Parties of India

In India, the Political Parties first appeared during the British rule. In 1885, the Indian National Congress (INC) came into existence and it was India's first political party. After that in 1906, the Indian Muslim League came into being. The Muslim League being the communal party of the Muslims, the Hindus in India established the Hindu Mahasabha in the year 1916. In the meantime after the Communist government was formed in 1917 in Russia, similar communist parties came to be formed in some other countries of the world. In India too, Indian Communist party was formed in 1924. Thereafter, many political parties came into existence and some of them disappeared too. Again some new parties are formed from some original political parties. Some regional parties have also come up after the national parties came into being. Among the existing political parties some of the all India national political parties are the following:

Indian National Congress (INC)

Popularly known as the Congress Party, it is one of the oldest political parties in the world. Founded in 1885 and has experienced many splits, it played a dominant role in Indian Politics at the national and state level for several decades after India's independence. Under the leadership of Jawaharlal Nehru, the party sought to build a modern secular democratic republic in India. Ruling party at the centre till 1977 and then from 1980 to 1989. After 1989, its support declined, but it continues to be present throughout the country, cutting across social divisions. A centrist party (neither rightist nor leftist) in its ideological orientation, the party espouses secularism and weaker and weaker sections and minorities. Supports new economic reforms but with a human face. Emerged as the largest party with 145 members in the Lok Sabha elections held in 2004 and led the United Progressive Alliance coalition government at the Centre (2004-14).

Bharatiya Janata Party (BJP)

Founded in 1980 by reviving the erstwhile Bharatiya Jana Sangh. Wants to build a strong and modern India by drawing inspiration from India's ancient culture and values. Cultural nationalism (or 'Hindutva') is an important element in its conception of Indian nationhood and politics. Wants full territorial and political integration of Jammu and Kashmir with India, a uniform civil code for all people living in the country irrespective of religion, and ban on religious conversions. Its support base increased substantially in the 1990s. Earlier limited to north and west and to urban areas, the party expanded its support in the south, east, the north-east and to the rural areas. Came to power in 1998 as the leader of the National Democratic Alliance including several state and regional parties. Lost elections in 2004 and is the principal opposition party in the Lok Sabha (2004-14). Came back to power in 2014 and is leading the National Democratic Alliance government at the Centre.

Bahujan Samaj Party (BSP)

Formed in 1984 under the leadership of Kanshi Ram. Seeks to represent and secure power for the Bahujan Samaj which includes the Dalits, Adivasis, OBCs, and the religious minorities. Draws inspiration from the ideas and teachings of Sahu Maharaj, Mahatma Phule, Periyar Ramaswami Naicker and Babasaheb Ambedkar. Stands for the cause of securing the interests and welfare of the dalits and oppressed people. It has its main base in the state of Uttar Pradesh and substantial presence in neighbouring states like Madhya Pradesh, Chattisgarh, Uttarakhand, Delhi and Punjab. Formed government in Uttar Pradesh several times by taking the support of different parties at different times. In the Lok Sabha elections held in 2004, it polled about 5 percent votes and secured 19 seats in the Lok Sabha.

Communist Party of India-Marxist (CPI-M)

Founded in 1964, the party believes in Marxism-Leninism. Supports socialism, secularism and democracy and opposes imperialism and communalism. Accept democratic elections as a useful and helpful means for securing the objective of socio-economic justice in India. Enjoys strong support in West Bengal, Kerala and Tripura, especially among the poor, factory workers, farmers, agricultural labourers and the intelligentsia. Critical of the new economic policies that allow free flow of foreign capital and goods into the country. Has been in power in West Bengal without a break for 30 years. In 2004 elections, it won about 6 percent of votes and 43 seats in the Lok Sabha. Currently supports the UPA from outside, without joining the government.

Communist Party of India (CPI)

Formed in 1925. Believes in Marxism-Leninism, secularism and democracy. Opposed to the forces of secessionism and communalism. Accepts parliamentary democracy as a means of promoting the interests of the working class, farmers and the poor. Became weak after the split in the party in 1964 that led to the formation of the CPI(M). Significant presence in the states of Kerala, West Bengal, Punjab, Andhra Pradesh and Tamil Nadu. Its support base had gradually declined over the years. It secured about 1.4 percent of votes and 10 seats in the 2004 Lok Sabha elections. Advocates the coming together of all left parties to build a strong left front. Currently supports UPA from outside.

Nationalist Congress Party (NCP)

Formed in 1999 following a split in the Congress party. Espouses democracy, Gandhian secularism, equity, social justice and federalism. Wants that high offices in government be confined to natural born citizens of the country. A major party in Maharashtra and has a significant presence in Meghalaya, Manipur and Assam. A coalition partner in the state of Maharashtra in alliance with the Congress. Since 2004, a member of the United Progressive Alliance.

Other than these six parties, most of the major parties of the country are classified by the Election Commission as "State Parties". These are commonly referred to as regional parties. Yet these parties need not be regional in their ideology or outlook. Some of these parties are all India parties that happen to have succeeded only in some states. Parties like the Samajwadi Party, Samata Party and Rashtriya Janata Dal have national level political organisation with units in several states. Some of these parties like Biju Janata Dal, Sikkim Democratic Front and Mizo National Front are conscious about their state identity. Over the last three decades, the number and strength of these parties has expanded. This made the Parliament of India politically more and more diverse. No one national party is able to secure on its own a majority in the Lok Sabha. As a result, the national parties are compelled to form alliance with state parties. Since 1996, nearly every one of the State parties has got an opportunity to be a part of one or the other national level coalition government. This has contributed to the strengthening of federalism and democracy in our country.

Some of the main regional parties which have come up in different regions similarly along with national parties are:- (a) Asom Gana Parishad (AGP) (b) Akali Dal (AD) (c) TeleguDesam Party (TDP) (d) Dravida Munnetra Kajhagam (DMK) (e) Anna Dravida Munnetra Kajhagam (ADMK) (f) National Conference, etc.

The all India parties work in most of the provinces of India and the regional parties work in their own regions. Among the regional political parties – Akali Dal (AD) in Punjab, Telegu Desam (TDP) in Andhra Pradesh, Dravida Munnetra Kajhagam (DMK) in Tamil Nadu and adjoining areas and National Conference in Jammu and Kashmir, have built up their working bases and followers and are engaged in the development of their regions.

Till 1976, the Indian National Congress (INC) had been forming government as the single majority party in the

Indian Parliament. But in 1977 for the first time, a non-congress government was formed at the centre under the banner of Janata party. In 1980, the Indian National Congress (INC) recaptured power at the centre under the leadership of Prime Minister Mrs. Indira Gandhi. Then afterwards for a few occasions no single party got majority for which coalition government was formed. Right now such coalition government is functioning under the banner of Indian National Congress and Bharatiya Janata Party simultaneously.

Role of Opposition in a Democracy

The role of opposition in a democracy is very significant. The parties which do not get chance to form government must keep constant vigil on the governance of the ruling majority party so that it cannot run a tyrranical rule. The opposition party must oppose if the government carries out anything unlawful. Especially the opposition parties must carry out wide and extensive publicity amongst the people against the activities of the ruling party which go beyond public interests. It must exert pressure on the government not to indulge in anti-welfare activities. The opposition parties have come to be recognized as indispensable organs of the democratic government for such a role. The opposition party appears to be very weak in case of India. The role of the opposition party was almost passive during the rule of the Indian National Congress in the early decades after India's independence. However when the hegemony of the Indian National Congress decreased considerably after the birth of the multi-party system and regional parties, the role of the opposition parties has increased manifold. The opposition party in

India has not been able to play a greater effective role for the reasons that these (parties) are divided among themselves and are not based on independent principles. The members of the opposition parties belonging to the union (central) and provincial (state) legislatures cannot oppose the government unitedly because of the differences in their party rules and principles. The opposition parties cannot adopt unanimous decisions on the issues and problems and hence they fail to guide the government in the right track by giving constructive and positive suggestions. For these reasons therefore, the role of the opposition parties in India has remained very weak till date.

Conclusion

Political party may be termed as the combination (conglomeration) of some people who organize themselves to work unitedly for the achievement of common objectives and having possessed similar opinion towards public issues and problems of the country. In the democratic system of administration, the administration of the country and the political activities are controlled by the political parties. Thus there is necessity to study about political parties. The first political party of India is the Indian National Congress. It was formed in 1885. The all India parties in the national level and the regional parties in the regional level work for the development of their own regions. The role of the opposition is very significant in democracy. In India, the opposition party is very weak. The opposition parties in India have not been able to play a significant role because they themselves are divided into many and they are based on different ideology and principles.

CHAPTER VII

Social Movements: Workers, Peasants, Environmental and Women's Movement

Workers and Peasants

Workers and Peasants in India have been involved in the collective actions in order to fight for their demands. Their collective actions like those of other social group can be included in the social and political movements. Workers and the peasants together form the largest groups of the Indian society. While the workers largely belong to the exploited section, the peasants consist of both the poor and the rich sections. These groups have been involved in the collective actions or the social and political movements to get their demand fulfilled. The nature of the issues raised by them or their leadership depends on the place they occupy in the economy or society. It also depends on the fact whether the workers are engaged in the organised, unorganised, agrarian or the industrial sectors or whether a peasant is a poor peasant or the rich peasant operating in the mechanised capitalist economy or in the backward –feudal economy. In this unit, we shall discuss important features of the workers and peasants movements in India.

Workers' Movements

The workers movement in India can be divided in two phases – the pre-Independence period and the post-Independence period.

Workers' Movements in the Colonial Period

The modern working class made its appearance in India in the second half of the 19th century with the growth of modern industries, railways, post and telegraph network, plantation and mining. But the labour movement started in an organised way only after the Second World War. The organised wokers' unions are known as the trade unions. The All India Trade Union Congress (A I T U C) was formed in 1920. Its objective was to coordinate activities of all organisations in all the provinces of India to further the interests of the Indian labour in economic, social and political matters. In the second half of the 1920s there was a consolidation of left ideological forces in the country. In 1928 the left wing including the communists succeeded in acquiring dominant position inside the A I T U C. The moderates started a new organisation known as All India Trade Union Federation (AITUF). The 1930s was not a favourable period for the growth of trade union movement India. The communists were implicated in the Meerut Conspiracy case and the Bombay Textiles strike of 1929 had failed. A lull marked the activities on the trade union front. The serious economic depression of this period added to the woes of the workers further. It led to large-scale retrenchment. The main focus of the trade union movements during this period was maintaining wages and preventing retrenchment. The Second World War divided the trade union leaders. The communists argued that with the Nazi attack on the Soviet Union in 1941 the character of the war had changed from imperialist war to people's war. The communists were following the line of the Russian Communist Party and thought that in the changed circumstances it was the duty of the workers to support British war efforts. But the nationalist leaders wanted to strengthen the national movement to overthrow the British rule from India. The ideological rift led to another split in the trade union movement. The mounting cost of living made the workers to realise the need of an organised effort to secure relief. In spite of the government resorting to Defence of India Rules, which prohibited strikes and lockouts, there was a perceptible increase in number of both unions and organised workers.

The Issues and the Types of Collective Actions

The main issues which caused the workers strikes include: wages, bonus, personnel, leave and hours of work, violence and indiscipline, industrial and labour policies, etc. The workers take recourse to various types of collective actions for getting their problems redressed. These are – strikes, satyagrah, hunger strikes, bandhs and hartals, gharaos, demonstrations, mass casual leaves, work to rule, cutting of supply of electricity, etc. The most common form of workers' collective action is the strike. There are examples of the railway, jute, plantation, mine and textiles workers strikes in the pre-Independence period. The centres of the strikes were Nagpur, Ahemadabad, Bombay, Madras, Howrah and Calcutta. In 1920 Gandhi intervened in the strike the textile workers of Ahmedabad and provided leadership to the workers.

Workers' Movements in the Post-colonial Period
(i) The National Level

The high hopes of workers were shattered after independence. There was hardly any improvement on the fronts of better wages and other service conditions. Three central trade union organisations were borne. The Indian National Trade Union Congress (INTUC) started by the Congress party was born in 1947. The Praja Socialist Party started the Hind Mazdoor Sabha (HMS) in 1948. The workers had to struggle hard even to retain what they had achieved earlier. A series of strikes stirred the country. There were highest number of strikes in 1947, i.e., 1811 strikes which involved 1840 thousand workers. The number of strikes and man-days lost had surpassed all the previous records. This declined in the 1950s, but number of strikes and lock-outs increased again in the 1960s-1970s. Some radicalists had formed the United Trade Union Congress (UTUC) in 1949. After 1964 when there was a division in the Communist Party of India and Communist Party of India (Marxist) was borne this led to a split in Communist controlled AITUC as well and in 1970 Centre for Indian Trade Union (C ITU) was borne. They are affiliated to the CPI and CMI (M). According to the provisional figures released by the Chief Labour Commissioner in 1994 Bharatiya Mazdoor Sangh (BMS) which is an affiliate of BJP has acquired a total membership of 31.17 lakh workers has secured the top position. The INTUC a Congress affiliated body with a total membership of 27.06 lakh is on the second position. The third position is enjoyed by CITU affiliated to CPM with a total membership of 17.98 lakh. The fourth position is enjoyed by HMS. According to the provisional figures the hold of Congress affiliated INTUC seems to have weakened. At the same time the hold of organisations like CITU, HMS and AITUC have strengthened.

(ii) The Provincial Levels

Another remarkable development of the 1960s was the birth of trade unions of the regional parties like the DMK and AIDMK in Madras. The Shiv Sena was born in Bombay in 1967. It soon set up its labour wing called Bharatiya Kamgar Sena. It was generally believed that the Shiv Sena had the backing of the industrial houses in the Bombay-Pune belt to counter the strong influence of the Communists and Socialists in labour unions. It succeeded in achieving this objective and its trade union established its supremacy in the Bombay region by the mid -1970s. The predominance of the Sena-led union was successfully challenged by Datta Samant, an eminent INTUC leader. When emergency was imposed in 1975 he refused to tone down his militancy. He was arrested and sent to jail. Then he was a Congress MLA. After coming out of jail when the emergency was lifted in 1977 he became even more popular. By the end of the 1970s he became the most powerful trade union leader in the Bombay-Pune belt. In the year 1978 he left both congress and the INTUC to set up an independent union named the Maharastra Girni Kamgar Union (MGKU). He remained one of the most influential trade union leader in Bombay till he was murdered.

(iii) The Trade Unions without Political Affiliations

The 1960s also witnessed the emergence of independent unions or "apolitical". They were independent in the sense that they were not affiliated to any political party or federation. These kinds of "apolitical" trade unions emerged out of the dissatisfaction of the workers with the existing trade unions which were affiliated to the political parties. The leadership of these unions has largely come from the educated middle classes. Engineering Mazdoor Sabha led by R J Mehta is one of the earliest unions of these type-covering workers in engineering, chemicals, printing and allied industries. Datta Samant started a number of unions like Association of Engineering workers, Mumbai General Kamgar Union, Maharashtra Girni Kamgar Union. Shankar Guha Neyogi and A.K. Roy also came into limelight as leaders of independent unions. Neyogi concentrated on contract workers in the iron–ore mines of Dalli Rajhara near Bhilai in Madhya Pradesh into a formidable union. While AITUC and INTUC were concerned with the problems of permanent and better paid workers of the Bhilai Steel Plant, concentrated on casual workers employed in small and medium-scale industries in the region. Neyogi was murdered in 1990. Another example of this type is A.K. Roy who organised coal mine workers in the Dhanbad-Jhariya belt of Bihar. Roy`s support base was also among contract and casual labour in the coalmines. Roy also received support from a large number of local tribal mine workers because the trade unions operating in these areas did not satisfy them. Another important example of this type was the Self- Employed Women's Association (SEWA) formed by Ela Bhat. She founded SEWA because she felt that unions in the organised sectors were not sensitive to the problems encountered by female workers. These are not the only examples of independent unions. One of the most important examples of the movement launched by the union which was unaffiliated to the political parties was the textile workers' strike of 1982 in Mumbai. Dissatisfied with the Rastriya Mill Mazdoor Sangh (RMMS), affiliated to the INTUC the workers of the textile industry in Mumbai, rallied behind the MGKU-led by Datta Samant. The workers of the textile workers of Mumbai went on indefinite strike on January 18, 1982. The demands of the workers included higher wages, making the badli (temporary) workers permanent, allowances for leave and travel and payment for house rent. The workers of other sectors than the textile also rallied behind Datta Samant. The Industrialists adopted intransigent attitude towards the strike. The strike created hardships for the workers. The strike had its repercussion on the rural areas to which the workers belonged. The textile workers also were the poor peasants or small farmers having links both in the cities as well the villages. Datta Samat was able to link the rural issues like the wages of agricultural labourer with those of the textile workers. The strike, however, did not succeed in getting the original demands of the workers accepted. But it helped Datta Samant to emerge as the most influential trade union leader in Bombay.

(iv) Limitations of the Trade Union Movement in India

The Trade Union Movement in India is faced with many defects. Only a small fraction of the working class is organised. Even in the organised sector a sizable chunk of workers do not participate in Trade Union Movement. Indian economy is largely agriculture based. Small peasants and agricultural labour encounter the problems of seasonal unemployment and low income. They are forced to go to cities in search of employment. Most of these workers are illiterate and ignorant and under the grip of superstitions and they have a migratory character. A large section of the workers do not exhibit much interest in trade union movement because city life for them is a temporary condition. So they do not realise the importance of unity among workers. Another major weakness of trade union is poor finance. This is a fact that working class in India is a very small part of the population but the main problem is the multiplicity of trade unions. The subscription rate by Indian workers is very less. This makes the trade unions dependent on external finance and influence. Yet another weakness of the trade union movement has been the dominance of the leadership from outside. The main reason for this has been lack of education among the workers. Mostly leadership is provided by professional politicians. It is being increasingly felt that the working class movement should be led by persons from the ranks of the workers who are aware of the problems and difficulties encountered by the working class. Political leadership ignores the needs and welfare of the workers and tries to use the organization for the interest of the political party.

Peasant Movements

Peasants are those agrarian classes which are related to agriculture as the tenants or owners of land and participate in the farming activities. They are a differentiated group. In the backward and feudal agriculture they cultivate land as the tenants of the landlords. In the more advanced agriculture, where the tenants have become the landowners following the implementation of the of the land reforms, they are the owners of the land. The peasants whose resources in the land are not enough to meet their basic needs and who also work as labourers for others apart from working on their fields are poor and small peasants. The peasants who do not work for wages, but have enough resources relating to agriculture are rich and middle peasants or the farmers. They either mainly depend on the family labour to work on the land or they may combine it with the hired labour from outside the family. In this section we will be studying the movements of the small and poor peasants as well those of the rich peasants or the farmers.

Small and Poor Peasant Movements

There were several peasant movements in Independence periods. Some examples of the former are – Oudh movement (UP) in 1920, Kheda and Bardoli (Guajarat) and Champaran (Bihar) movements and Moplah rebillions. The main examples of the of the post-Independence period are – Telangana (Andhra Pradesh), and Tibhaga and Naxalite (West Bengal) movements. The peasants during the pre-Independence period were living in economic conditions. They were exploited by a group of classes, e.g. landlords and their agents, moneylenders and the officials of the colonial state. The landlords increased the rents on the peasants continuously, took forced gifts and extracted begar from them. The inability of the peasants to pay these multiplied due to the frequent famines and draught which affected them adversely. They were heavily indebted to the moneylenders in order to pay the rent and meet the needs of their subsistence. When the peasants could not pay the rent, services or the begar, they were evicted form their land. They were also physically tortured. Commercialisation of crops and introduction of new land rules further worsened their conditions. The peasants reacted to by revolting against the landlords, moneylenders and agents of the some organisation. In case there was no organisation, the century different political parties mobilised the radical nationalists and many leaders of peasant colonial state. Leadership in the peasant movements was provided either by the rural intelligentsia or urban intelligentsia. Baba Ram Chand, the leader of the Oudh peasant movement belonged to the former. The peasants had been mobilised by some kind of informal networking of the peasants and their leaders had worked as orgnisation. This was true especially for the localised revolts. The informal networking or the organisational structure worked in mobilisation, communication of the messages and in planning strategies and programmes. From the beginning of the twenties peasants in the revolts. The Congress started mobilising the peasants from the 1920s with the purpose to broaden its support base. This enabled peasant movements which were localised and running parallel to the national movement to merge with the latter. The Bardoli Sataygrah of 1928, no- rent campaign were examples of such merger. But the Congress did not encourage the conflict between the landlords and the peasants to get sharpened. The Congress had been more interested in forging an alliance between the landlords, peasants and other classes. After the Civil Disobedience Movement started sharing the impression that the Congress was sympathetic towards the capitalists and Zamindars. The need to evolve independent class organisations and leadership to safeguard the interest of the peasants was being felt by them. This was under these circumstances that the first all India peasant organisation, the All India Kisan Sabha was formed in 1936 in Lucknow under the presidentship of Swami Sahjanand Saraswati, the founder of Bihar Pradesh Kisan Sabha. N.G. Ranga, the pioneer of Kisan movement in Andhra became its first General Secretary. The birth of an all India organization with a programme of common demands and expressing the aspirations of the peasants all over the country was an event of great historical significance. Very soon the branches of the All India Kisan Sabha were established in many districts. The formation of Congress Ministries in a majority of the provinces in early 1937 marked the beginning of a new phase in the growth of peasant movements. The Congress had promised radical improvement in the conditions of the peasants on the eve of elections. There was definite increase in civil liberties, which provided better opportunities for the mobilization of peasantry. Different Congress Ministries introduced agrarian legislations for debt relief, restoration of lands lost during depression, for security of tenure etc. But these measures did not affect the conditions of the peasants of lower strata. The dissatisfaction of peasants found expression in a number of protest meetings, conferences and demonstrations. They criticised number of anti-peasant measures taken by the government like arrest of peasant leaders and banning peasant meetings. The outbreak of the World War II brought the resignation of the Congress Ministries and launching of severe repression against Kisan Sabha leaders. In the year 1939 the national convention of the All India Kisan Sabha was presided over by Acharya Narendra Dev. In his Presidential address he emphasised the need of separation of Kisan Sabha from Congress. According to him a separate Kisan Sabha was necessary in order to put pressure on the Congress. The end of the war, followed by the negotiation for the transfer of power and the anticipation of freedom marked a new stage in the history of peasant movements. Approaching freedom had filled the peasant movements with new spirit to assert their rights. The analysis of some of these movements gives us sufficient insight into the nature, social basis, achievements and limitations of the peasant movements in India. The Tebhaga Movement of Bengal was one of such movements. The provincial Kisan Sabha of Bengal launched this Movement in 1946. Gradually the influence of the left in general and the communists in particular increased in the Kisan Sabha. In 1947 the leadership of the All India Kisan Sabha went into the hands of the communists. The communists led the provincial Kisan Sabha of Bengal also. This Movement soon took the form of a clash between the bargardars (share-croppers) and the jotedars, the employers. The share-croppers began to assert that they would no longer pay a half share of their crop to their jotedars but only one- third. They also insisted that before division the crop would be stored in their khamars (godowns) and not in that of the jotedars. Poor peasants, middle peasants and also some sons of jotedars led the movement. The middle peasants provided the bulk of the leaders and they supported the movement up to the end. They hoped that it would culminate in total attack on landlordism. The rich peasants slowly detached themselves. When the government resorted to severe repression in 1947 the movement came to an end. Another such movement was the Telangna Movement. It was launched in 1946 in the princely state of Hyderabad ruled by the Nizam. This movement developed in the context of the post-war economic crisis. This movement started as a protest against collection of excessive revenue using force by jagirdars. In the beginning, the leadership was in the hands of the rich peasants and the movement was directed against the big absentee landlords allied to the Nizamsahi. But very soon the initiative passed into the hands of poor peasants and agricultural labour that started occupying lands of landlords and wastelands and started distributing it among them. By 1947, this movement organized a Guerilla Army mobilizing poor peasantry and agricultural labour many of which were tribal and untouchables. This army snatched large quantity of arms from the zamindars and drove away the local government officials. They established their control over an area of 15,000 square miles with a population of 40,000. The administrations in these areas were run by peasant soviets. The army of independent India succeeded in crushing the Telangna Movement in 1951. In 1967 there started a peasant protest at a place called Naxalbari in the Darjeeling District of West Bengal. After two decades of independence and congress rule there was disenchantment among people on a large scale, which found expression in Congress losing election in eight states. But the communists had done well in both Kerala and West Bengal. The per capita income was on decline and unemployment was on the rise. A group of young communists due to theoretical disputes resulting from the split of the Communist Party of India in 1964 protested CPIM's policy of participation in 1967 election and joining the government afterwards instead emphasised the need of armed struggle with peasantry as the leading element. The peasant organisation of the CPIM in Darjeeling district was in the hands of such communist leaders. The land reform policy of the government had not succeeded in taking lands from zamindars and big farmers and distributing among poor peasants and landless labour in any significant way. There existed discontent among peasants. In such situation, the leaders of peasant organization gave a call for establishing the government of peasant committees, organizing armed struggle to end the ownership of the jotedars on land and distribute it among poor peasants and landless labour. They drew inspiration from the Telangna Movement. The Naxalbari movement reached its zenith by the third week of May 1967. There was violence on a large scale. Naxalbari got enormous publicity largely because it was fighting a state government wherein CPIM was a major coalition partner and also because China believed that the

Naxalites were following the correct line. It lasted for fifty-two days only. In July 1967, police and battalions of paramilitary forces sent by Ajoy Mukherjee, then the Chief Minister of the state, combed the whole area and the rebellion was suppressed. Naxalbari was a minor event in terms of its durations, intensity of resistance; area controlled or number of casualties suffered or inflicted on the other side. On these indicators Telangna was a much bigger happening. But Naxalbari acquired the symbol of armed peasant uprising. It had its reverberations all over the country. After this the revolutionaries who became active in U.P., Bihar, Punjab, Kashmir, Kerala and Andhra Pradesh came to be known as Naxalites. It emerged as a more powerful force in Kerala, Andhra Pradesh and Bihar. The emergence of Naxalism led to the formation of C.P.I. (Marxist Leninist) the third Communist party. This party believed that the goal of socialism could be achieved through armed struggle, justified use of violence for capturing lands of Zamindars and distributing them among poor peasants. The Naxalite Movement became a reference point for those poor peasants and landless labour that got nothing from the government except promises and whose condition showed no signs of improvement and were suffering oppressions at the hands of rural dominant sections. They found a ray of hope in this militant philosophy. This philosophy continues to inspire that segment of rural population who has lived at the receiving end. At many places, they are fighting for security of employment, minimum wages, rights over a share of produce and against sexual abuse of their women. There are instances of violence when they exercise their right to vote. Most of the time they have to resort to violence to protect their rights and dignity which is under threat from the land owning and dominant sections of society. Their faith in violence is strengthened because they find the state and the police always taking sides with the land owning dominant sections of society. The second phase of land reforms known as the Land Ceiling Act started from 1961 onwards with the stated objective of distributing land among the landless. After the Naxalbari Movement of 1967 and the Land Grab Movements launched in different states of 1970 the need to impose rigorous land ceiling was realized. As early as in 1969 the Home Minister had warned that if steps were not taken to lessen agrarian tension both by the state and central government things would go beyond control. Land Reforms was essential part of the twenty Point Programme of Mrs Indira Gandhi during Emergency period. But in spite of all this by 1977, only 4.04 million acres were declared surplus, out of this 2.10 million were taken over by the government and merely 1.29 million acres were actually distributed. The much acclaimed Green Revolution did not make much of difference in their condition. The percentage of households below poverty line in the rural areas has gone up from 38.11% in 1960-61 to 48% in 1977-78. Agricultural labour continues to be their main income and most of the studies suggest that there has been a marked decline in both real wages and the days of work. Naxalite outfits are active in Andhra Pradesh, Bihar, Madhya Pradesh and also in newly created states of Jharkhand and Chatisgarh. Many times they indulge in mindless militancy but they continue to inspire the underdogs of rural society because mostly they take up the problems faced by these sections. The government treats their armed struggle as law and order problem and uses police and paramilitary forces to suppress them. The government has not shown the determination to address to the problems faced by the rural poor. The land reforms carried out by the government had not succeeded in distributing land among poor peasants and landless labour in any significant way. There have been attempts to ameliorate the financial conditions of poor peasants, agricultural labourers and artisans in the rural areas through funds made available by the central governments to the districts. But a major chunk of these funds are cornered by local vested interests. The agricultural labourers, poor peasants, contract labourers whether dalits, tribals or caste Hindus have been struggling to assert their rights. They struggle for wages, land and against oppression of different types. Their movements are weak and divided. But surely it has a potential to emerge as a powerful force and can get justice.

Rich Peasants' and Farmers' Movements

The last quarter of the twentieth century has seen the movements of a very important social group in the rural areas known as rich peasants, farmers, kulaks or the capitalist farmers in several regions of India. They rallied behind the farmers' organisations in their respective regions. These organisations are - two Bharatiya Kisan Unions (the BKUs) of Punjab and Uttar Pradesh, Shetkari Sangathan of Maharastra, Khadyut Samaj of Gujarat, Karnataka Rjya Raitha Sangha of Karnartaka and Vivasayigal of Tamil Nadu. The most prominent leaders of these unions are Bhupendra Singh Mann in Punjab, Mahendra Singh Tikait in UP, Sharad Joshi in Maharastra and Nandunjappa Swami in Karnatak. These farmers are the most influential and resourceful sections of rural society in their respective regions. They largely belong to the intermediate castes. They have benefited most from the state policies especially the land reforms and the green revolution. They cultivate land with the family labour supported by the hired-labour. They control the maximum resources in the rural society – land, water resources, animals, modern technology like tractors, etc. The movements of rich farmers unlike the movements of poor peasants are not directed against any rural exploiters. In fact, a large group of them belong to the latter. These are directed against the state and unequal terms of trade. Their main demands have been – remunerative prices, susidised imputs, writing off loans, lowering of electricity bills, substantial reduction in water canal charges, representation of the farmers in the Agricultural Price Commission. With the exception of the Maharastra, these movement did not raise the problems of the small producers. Rather, Tikait has demanded scrapping of land ceiling laws and of the Minimum wages Act. The most common mode of mobilisation in the farmers' or the rich peasants' movements include rallies, satyagrah, road blocaked, gaon bandi (banning the entry of outsiders into the villages) and attack on the public property. Some times these result in violence. Their "apolitical" nature, which means their not being attached to the political parties has been the most effective method of mobilisation, especially in the in the initial phase of the movements. While the farmers' movements in India shared several common characteristics, e.g. they raised the market-oriented demands, their "apolitical" nature, their direction against the state, patterns of mobilisation, the BKU movement of UP was distinct in terms of leadership and involvement of the traditional institution. Mahendra Singh Tikait, the chief of the Uttar Pradesh BKU is also the hereditary head of the traditional caste organisation known as the Sarva Khap of the farming Jats. His social position enabled him to become the leader of the BKU at a time when the farmers of the UP did not have a leader of that stature in the wake of the death of Charan Singh in 1987. Tikait was able to involve the traditional leaderships or Khaps-chiefs of several farming castes under the banner of the BKU. Besides, the BKU also took up the social issues like dowry in the initial phase of its movement. The Bharatiya Kissan Union of Mahendra Singh Tikait speaks a language that invokes elements of Charan Singh's discourse on agriculture. Charan Singh used to argue that there was an urban bias in Indian planning and held it accountable for diversion of resources from agriculture. It, however, does not go to the extent of treating industrial and urban India agains the rural India unlike the Shetkari Sangathan of Sharad Joshi. The rich peasant organisations do not admit any contradiction between the interests of rich peasants and the poor agrarian classes. They argue that unremunerative prices affect both the rich and the poor peasants. While the Shetkari Sangthan maintains a façade of India and Bharat divide to hide the class divide in agriculture, the BKU conceals it under the cover of existing Bhaichara (brotherhood) and peasant-proprietorship in the western U.P. The movement of rich peasant has become an important fact of the present day Indian reality. No political party can afford to displease them. The government's decision to enhance electricity rates for farmers, raising fertilizer prices are met with stiff resistance. Many times they resort to stoppage of the supply of commodities like onion, sugar or milk to get their demands conceded. One thing has become obvious that there has been a tremendous increase in the power of this class. They not only exploit the labour power and control majority of land, they also control levers of power like gram panchayat, zila parishad co-operatives and educational institutions and banks to get maximum benefit from these institution and also to maintain its dominant position in the rural area. The rich farmers are diversifying their sources of income. Some of their income comes from outside the agrarian sector like employment in cities, rent trade, money lending or transport. They are also investing in small industries like sugar and rice mills as well as in food processing.

The Impact of Economic Liberalization on the Workers and Peasants Movements

The economic reforms in the country that came to be known as liberalisation can be said to be mainly the - 1990 development. The era of reforms started with the government of P.V. Narsimha Rao. Since then successive governments have continued with liberalisation agenda. The present government of Atal Behari Vajpayee is also committed to this agenda. Among the main planks of this New Economic Policy are closure of sick and loss making public enterprises, disinvestments from and privatisation of the public sector enterprises. There has been a marked decline in the growth rate of total employment in the organised sector in the 1990`s as compared to 1980`s. In fact this period is known as a period of jobless growth. Labour laws relating to job security are being changed. Many workers have been pushed out of jobs under the voluntary retirement scheme. A practice of using contract and casual labour in place of regular employees has become widespread. There have been strikes by Trade Unions to protect the interests of workers in State Electricity Boards,

ITDC hotels, banks, etc. A National Renewal Fund was created as early as in 1992 to provide a social safety net to the labour force rendered jobless. In 1994, the government of India signed the Uruguway round of the General Agreement on Tariffs and Trade (GATT) at Maracas [Morocco] and became a member of the World Trade Organization (WTO). This step of the government can be seen as part of the New Economic Policy. As per conditions of the GATT, developing countries including India are under obligation to introduce subsidies-discipline. They are being asked to keep subsidies to the farmers up to 10% of their value of output. But cutting down on subsidies is a difficult proposition because no government wants to displease the rich farmers. They continue to get things like irrigation waters and electricity either free or at throwaway prices. Another GATT related problem faced by the farmers is introduction of patenting in agriculture. The farmer is not automatically permitted to use farm-saved-seeds of protected varieties to sow the next crop. He has either to pay compensation for the use of seeds saved by him or obtain the approval of the breeder. As most of the Plant Breeders are the Multi National Corporations (MNCs), their primary intention is maximisation of profit. This leaves the farmers no option, but to buy the seeds again. Farmers in Karnataka attacked the farm of Cargill Seeds to register their anger. There have been protests against Terminator Seeds of cotton in Maharashtra and Gujrat. The response of the rich farmers' movements to new developments like the New Economic Policy, India joining WTO has not been undifferentiated. While Sharad Joshi in the western part of the country has supported the new developments. Mahendra Singh Tikait in the north and Nanjundaswamy in the south have been critical of it.

In this unit, we have studied about the collective action or the social and political movements of the workers and the peasants in India. These groups have been agitating from the colonial period for the redressal of their grievances. They formed their organisations and responded to the call of their leadership. The problems of the workers included mainly wages, bonus, personnel, leave and hours of work, violence and indiscipline, industrial and labour policies, etc. The peasants are not a homogeneous category. The poor and small peasants are related to their vulnerable social and economic conditions. The farmers which are also known as the rich peasants, kulaks or the capitalist farmers are mobilised around the issues related to the developed and commercial farming. The period from the 1970s onwards has seen the rise of workers and peasants' organisations and the movements which are not affiliated to any political party. The farmers and peasants movements affect the political processes in India to a significant extent.

Environmental Movements

An environmental movement is a type of social movement that involves an array of individuals, groups and coalitions that perceive a common interest in environmental protection and act to bring about changes in environmental policies and practices. Environmental and ecological movements are among the important examples of the collective actions of several social groups.

Cause of Environmental Movements

The increasing confrontation with nature in the form of industrial growth, degradation of natural resources, and occurrence of natural calamities, has resulted in imbalances in the bio-spheric system.

Major reasons for the emergence of environmental movements in India are as follows:

(i) Control over natural resources

(ii) False developmental policies of the government

(iii) Right of access to forest resources

(iv) Non-commercial use of natural resources

(v) Social justice/human rights

(vi) Socioeconomic reasons

(vii) Environmental degradation/destruction and

(viii) Spread of environmental awareness and media

Major Environmental Movements in India

Many environmental movements have emerged in India, especially after the 1970s. These movements have grown out of a series of independent responses to local issues in different places at different times.

Some of the best known environmental movements in India have been briefly described below:

The Silent Valley Movement

The silent valley is located in the Palghat district of Kerala. It is surrounded by different hills of the State. The idea of a dam on the river Kunthipuzha in this hill system was conceived by the British in 1929. The technical feasibility survey was carried out in 1958 and the project was sanctioned by the Planning Commission of the Government of India in 1973. In 1978, the movement against the project from all corners was raised from all sections of the population. The movement was first initiated by the local people and was subsequently taken over by the Kerala Sastra Sahitya Parishad (KSSP). Many environmental groups like the Narmada Bachao Andolan (NBA), Bombay Natural History Society (BNHS) and Silent Valley Action Forum participated in the campaign.

The Silent Valley Movement – Quick Facts

Year of the Movement 1978

Place Kerala

Leaders Kerala Sastra Sahitya Parishad (KSSP) and local people

Reason/Aim of the Movement To save the silent valley and its rich biodiversity from the hydroelectric dam project that had been proposed.

Chipko Movement

Chipko Movement started on April 24, 1973, at Mandal of Chamoli district of Gharwal division of Uttarakhand. The Chipko is one of the world-known environmental movements in India. The movement was raised out of ecological destabilisation in the hills. The fall in the productivity of the forest produces forced the hill dwellers to depend on the market, which became a central concern for the inhabitants. Forest resource exploitation was considered the reason behind natural calamities like floods, and landslides. On March 27 the decision was taken to 'Chipko" that is 'to hug' the trees that were threatened by the axe and thus the chipko Andolan (movement) was born. This form of protest was instrumental in driving away the private companies from felling the ash trees.

Chipko Movement – Quick Facts

Year of the Movement 1973

Place Uttarakhand

Leaders Chandi Prasad Bhatt, Sunderlal Bhaguna and others

Reason/Aim of the Movement To protect the Himalayan forests from destruction

Bishnoi Movement

This movement was led by Amrita Devi, in which around 363 people sacrificed their lives for the protection of their forests. This movement was the first of its kind to have developed the strategy of hugging or embracing the trees for their protection spontaneously.

Bishnoi Movement – Quick Facts

Year of the Movement 1700s

Place Rajasthan

Leaders Amrita Devi Bishnoi

Reason/Aim of the Movement To stop the destruction of the village's sacred trees for building a new palace for the king

Appiko Movement

It is a movement inspired by the Chipko movement by the villagers of Western Ghats. In the Uttar Kannada region of Karnataka, the villagers of Western Ghats started the Appiko Chalewali movement during the month of September – November 1983. Here, the destruction of forest was caused due to commercial felling of trees for timber extraction. Natural forests of the region were felled by the contractors, which resulted in soil erosion and drying up of perennial water resources. In the Saklani village in Sirsi, the forest dwellers were prevented from collecting usufructs like twigs and dried branches and non-timber forest products for the purposes of fuelwood, fodder, honey etc. They were denied their customary rights to these products. In September 1983, women and youth of the region decided to launch a movement similar to Chipko, in South India. The agitation continued for 38 days, and this forced the state government to finally concede to their demands and withdraw the order for the felling of trees.

Appiko Movement – Quick Facts

Year of the Movement 1983

Place Karnataka

Leaders Panduranga Hegde, Villagers of Western Ghats; Women and youth from Saklani and surrounding villages

Reason/Aim of the Movement To stop cutting trees by the fellers and the contractors of the forest department. The people demanded a ban on the felling of green trees.

Narmada Bachao Andolan

Narmada is one of the major rivers of the Indian Peninsula. The scope of the Sardar Sarovar project, a terminal reservoir on Narmada in Gujurat in fact is the main issue in the Narmada Water dispute.

Narmada Bachao Andolan – Quick Facts

Year of the Movement 1985

Place Gujarat, MadhyaPradesh and Maharashtra

Leaders Medha Patkar and other activists

Reason/Aim of the Movement To question the rationale behind the developmental projects, especially dam construction across the river.

Jungle Bachao Andolan

Jungle Bachao Andolan began in the 1980s in the Singhbhum district of Bihar (presently in Jharkhand). It was a movement against the government's decision to grow commercial teak by replacing the natural Sal forests. The tribal community is the most affected by this decision as it disturbs the rights and livelihood of Adivasis of that region. This movement was widely spread in states like Bihar, Jharkhand and Odisha in various other forms.

Jungle Bachao Andolan – Quick Facts

Year of the Movement 1982

Place Singhbhum district of Bihar (now Jharkhand)

Leaders Tribals of Singhbhum

Reason/Aim of the Movement To oppose the government's decision to replace natural Sal forest with commercial teak plantations.

Women's Movements

The term "women's movement" does not refer to any one single, unified movement or entity. It is made of several movements based on a wide range of issues. It involves using of different approaches at various points of time. It is a term used in recognition of the "feel that all these movements" are working in some way or the other towards the emancipation of women.

These movements aim at reformulation of public life, the educational sphere, the workplace and the home; in short, they aim at total transformation of society. Women's movements can be termed as conscious and collective movements that try to deal with a set of problems and needs specific to women. These needs or problems are, in turn, created by a socio-cultural system that categorically puts them at a disadvantage in comparison to men.

According to Rajendra Singh, any theoretical perspective for studying women's movements and their strategy should include the following propositions:

In general, resistance and protests against unjust structures of power and the institutions of patriarchy and patriarchal oppression of women begins with the oppressions themselves. These oppressions are ever-present and ubiquitous (widespread).

Conscious rejection of injustice and resistance to the practices of oppression generally pass through phases of open manifestation of resistance and latent phases (when overt resistance is not visible). These phases depend upon the historical experiences of societies.

These forms of resistance—manifest and latent—determine the methods, strategies and techniques adopted by women to fight for their identity, dignity, self-defence and social justice. Sometimes, women's movements contain a "zone of silent war" waged by women to gain control over men in everyday life.

Women have put up resistance because of generally silent and unorganized disenchantments, suppressed feelings of rejection and of gender injustice in the patriarchal societies. These factors have led women to oppose erosion of identity at an individual level and can result in an organized outburst taking the form of manifest women's movements.

They may remain dormant in terms of organized movements, but active at the individual level and make a conscious use of a whole range of methods such as arts, ruses and moves against men. These methods are generally practised by women on men for coping with the day-to-day situations of oppression.

For any individual resistance to become an organized open movement, it has to pass through different stages of maturation. This process involves sharing of individual experiences of resistance with other individuals who are placed in similar life situations. This also includes a phase where the resistance is made obvious or becomes an exterior issue and a collective group emerges.

An ideology that rejects the negatively defined authority, leadership, mobilization and communication emerges. The progress from an unorganized and silent individual resistance to an open and organized women's movement is uneven and difficult. It is also difficult for an individual resistor to become a part of an organized movement.

In the everyday life situations of women in the male-dominated world of most contemporary societies, the art of resistance at the individual level, as well as organized collective movements coexist and even work simultaneously, though they may be conflicting practices and processes.

The women's studies of the 1970s and 1980s shifted focus from the perspective of family, marriage, socialization or social status to treating them as autonomous human beings. The emphasis today is on women's identity, consciousness, their subjectivity and the bio-psychological foundations of their personality.

CHAPTER VIII

Strategies in India since Independence: Planned Economy and Neo Liberalism

Introduction

When India attained Independence in 1947, a changeover in the Indian economy was really long overdue to meet the difficulties of modernity. Right after increasing Independence the main challenges facing the Indian economy was modernisation and for that setting up of contemporary industries was experienced when the demand of the hour. India took to the road of economic planning for this after April 1, 1951 influenced by the experience of the erstwhile Soviet economic planning like a number of other nations at that time of time. The report uses a number of vital commentary on India's neoliberalism conveyed in the type of the so-called New Economic Policy. It argues, New Economic Policy is actually a lot more when compared to a governmental policy. Neo-liberalism is actually applied through, as well as entails, the transformation of room, and hence creates overwhelming spatial unevenness. Neo-liberalism is as well a part of the imperialist task.

India Wins Freedom on 15 August 1947, Nehru had declared: "Long years ago we launched a trust with destiny, and today the time comes when we shall redeem the pledge of ours. The achievement we celebrate these days is actually though a phase, an opening of opportunity, to the fantastic triumph as well as achievements that await us." He reminded the nation that the responsibilities ahead included "the ending of ignorance and poverty & inequality and sickness of opportunity". These had been the fundamental foundations on which India embarked upon the path of its improvement since increasing independence in 1947. The goal of this paper is actually analysing just how much has India actually achieved within the last seventy years in fulfilling the aspirations on which it was founded.

The British handed over to free India, an economy filled with distortions as well as imbalances. reeling in the burden of stagnation, in consequence of the perpetuation of primarily pre-capitalist modes of generation both in farming and industry and also the colonial pattern of international trade. Impartial India, was, therefore confronted with issues that were formidable in nature and gigantic in magnitude. The land was practically in the grip of economic stagnation, poverty that is prevalent, unemployment and also the consequent human misery. The stagnating agricultural industry had to be converted to usher in an era of countryside prosperity. The backwards manufacturing industry had to reformed for creating a good and self-reliant economy. The partition of the nation had even more aggravated the economic crisis. The economy was nearly a century behind the innovative manufacturing nations of the planet. So it started to be important that measures be taken to remedy the ills of the economy as well as work made to set it on the right' - road of sustained progress had to attain inside a really brief span of time, the amount of improvement which the then developed nations of the planet got a century or even much more to achieve below favorable factors. It had been within these powerful forces which India formulated a selection of policies for brief economic growth as well as economic development.

For many part of the original years after independence disruptions connected with partition, drafting a constitution as well as the establishment of a brand new government, etc. occupied the main interest of the Indian leaders. The very first main undertaking of the very first democratic government under Prime Minister Jawaharlal Nehru was formulating an improvement technique to change India's economy from a dismal status following the exploitative colonial rule to a self-contained economy, and thereby, initiate a process of rapid as well as healthy economic development. In order to purport its improvement, approach the Government of India set up the Planning Commission in 1950 underneath the chairmanship of the Prime Minister, and that is the main bureau to design, execute as well as keep track of the 5 Year Plans (FYP).

Strategies in India since Independence: Planned Economy and Neo Liberalism

The goal of India's development strategy has been establishing a socialistic pattern of modern society through economic development with self-reliance, social justice as well as elimination of poverty. These goals had been to be accomplished to a democratic political framework making use of the mechanism of a diverse economy in which each private and public sectors co-exist. India initiated planning for national economic improvement with the establishment of the Planning Commission. The goal of the very first 5 Year Plan (1951-56) was raising domestic savings for development as well as in order to assist the economy resurrect itself from colonial rule. The actual rest with the past in planning arrived with the next 5 Year Plan (Nehru Mahalanobis Plan). The industrialization approach articulated by Professor Mahalanobis placed focus on the improvement of quite heavy industries and envisaged a dominant role for the public sector of the economy. The entrepreneurial job of the state was evoked to produce the manufacturing sector. Commanding heights of the economy had been entrusted to the public sector. The goals of manufacturing policy were: a higher growth rate, national self-reliance, reduction of international dominance, building up of indigenous capability, encouraging tiny scale sector, bringing about healthy regional growth, prevention of focus of economic power, reduction of earnings inequalities as well as command of economy by the State. The planners as well as policy makers recommended the demand for making use of a range of instruments as condition allocation of investment, licensing along with other regulatory controls to steer Indian manufacturing development on a closed economy foundation.

Major Objectives of the Indian Planning Process

Right after increasing Independence the main challenges facing the Indian economy was modernisation and for that setting up of contemporary industries was experienced when the demand of the hour. India took to the road of economic planning for this after April 1, 1951 influenced by the experience of the erstwhile Soviet economic planning like a number of other nations at that time of time. Nevertheless, Indian planning was distinct from the Soviet one as India's was a signs planning activity even though the Soviet planning was essential in fashion provided the political framework of its from which India differed considerably.

The main goals of the Indian planning had been four fold - (a) growth, (b) modernisation, (c) self-reliance, and (d) social justice or perhaps equity. Of all these, modernisation as well as self-reliance received probably the most interest in the original days of planning with the perception that setting up of contemporary industries as well as infrastructure would instantly take proper care of social justice and economic growth as the advantages of industrialisation and concomitant economic growth would trickle down to the marginal areas of the populations. The onus of industrialisation largely fell on the shoulder of the public sector which was imminent in the next Industrial Policy Resolution in 1956. The ideal of self-reliance was pursued in phrases of import substitution led industrialisation path along with a bit of pessimism for exports of the original days. The rules as well as regulations had been slowly set up appropriately to allow for some regime where state used to play the main role straight in phrases of productive activities as well as in terms of intervening in the performance of market.

There seemed to be a debate of Indian means of economic development through state led industrialisation and import substitution. Probably the most important critique of India's planning for industrialisation was Jagdish Bhagwati that in 1970 experienced the road chosen by India was an incorrect one as it will obstruct the performance of market place that is free and would instil hence inefficiency in the device in the neoclassical feeling of the phrase.

The primary objective of planning, consequently, was to diversify India's output base as well as to quickly industrialise the nation; "to build up the country of ours industrially and bring about in fact that long deferred industrial revolution in this particular country." (Nehru, quoted in Nayyar 1972). The planners needed to envision India from as a "poor, fairly fixed, mainly agricultural as well as conventional economy" to as an economy which would be "richer, powerful, modern and industrial."

In a nutshell, the post Independent switch of India may best be characterised by one of remarkable economic development as compared to the colonial past of its as well as, amazing improvement of capital items sector as well as public sector dominated manufacturing sector and a nationalised as well as healthy economic industry coupled with quite unimpressive improvement in living standards of typical individuals as well as health and education public. Some (tribal and bad agricultural folks) had been displaced from their livelihood and land to generate "sacrifice" for economic growth along with a labour force divided between informal and formal setting of the economy.

Concept of Neo-Liberalism in Planning Strategies

Neoliberalism demands a smaller government with a tax system a lot as well as considerable generous for the corporate and rich on the one hand as well as smaller government expenditure. The latter means in fact decrease in interpersonal sector expenditure as well as subsidies in relative sense. Being a result, the Government had to carry out the Fiscal Responsibility as well as Budget Management Act to discipline the very own fiscal practice of its that is currently put on quite possibly by the various State Governments. Thus, the strain on the Government is currently on to consist of fiscal deficit. On the other hand, the single goal of the Monetary Policy remains one of inflation targeting and so as to be sure that the actual price return doesn't fall under the threshold limit. This particular goal of monetary policy is actually little doubt associated with the motive of speculative finance which often would like to guarantee a threshold actual return on assets. On the one hand, the financial reforms are actually making rooms for speculative finance of the nation as may be noticed in phrases of raising derivative and commodity trading as well as booms in stock markets. On the other hand, the onus of trying to keep the investor's wellness unchanged has befallen today on monetary expert in phrases of inflation targeting which takes inflation as a clean monetary trend in a nation as India characterized by a lot of need and supply-side bottlenecks. And so, neoliberalism has produced the own tension of it's for the monetary and fiscal policy regime to accommodate the curiosity of capital and finance at the price of work. There's in fact redistribution of assets to capital owning category as well as the allies of its in the liberalised economic industry of the progression.

Neo-liberal economic liberalisation hence discovered changes in policy stance that is economic in each monetary and fiscal policy matters. With the government introducing self-control on fiscal deficit through Fiscal Responsibility and Budget Management Act to consist of fiscal deficit, the fiscal policy alternative of boosting government expenditure, flat when needed, is actually gone. At exactly the same time, this's a stage which witnessed overwhelming concessions or maybe financial assistance provided to the capital at the price of work to draw in private - especially foreign investment. The state laws as well as controls in sector had been transformed to facilitate the market led expansion of industries. The monetary policy on the additional hand became a lot more focused on inflation targeting. As compared to the earlier period of post Independent planning as well as state led transition, this particular stage of transition registered a lot more remarkable economic growth rates before remained very unthinkable. Gone are actually the days of what's widely known as Hindu Rate of Growth, the phrase coined by Raj Krishna to explain the reasonable growth documents of the planning days. The pose of economic planning even went by transformation with express led funding targeting no longer staying the process of planning. If the Eighth Plan began in 1992, the question was raised about the explanation for economic planning of a market-friendly liberalised economy. The Planning Commission came out naturally with the perception that planning will be henceforth for sticking to the interpersonal goals which hitherto stayed not a lot of target oriented in the Indian planning exercise. And so, on the one hand the market will stay in charge of cultivating funding as well as the state and capital development would while facilitating the development of a market that is free stay concentrated on a number of distribution policies targeting the interpersonal sectors like education, health, poverty alleviation, employment generation for the disadvantaged and poor, minority and scheduled caste/scheduled females and tribe as well as kids etc. A brand new idea was fitted in the idea of planning in India viz. monitor able targets, in which particular ph levels of targets will be repaired for interpersonal indicators (say, infant mortality rate) to be accomplished to a certain time period. Resources will be appropriately allocated under various state sponsored programmes in the implementation part of which regional self-governments viz. citified municipalities as well as village Panchayats would perform better role.

Planning of Economy after Independence Strategies

The Economic Policy is not simply a government policy, and it's neither completely new or just economic. Formally released in 1991, it essentially presents the needs of the capitalist class, and much more specifically, the demands of hegemonic fractions of the foreign-diasporic and domestic capitalist class at a specific phase in the improvement of Global and Indian capitalism. The Economic Policy seeks to produce conditions where foreign and domestic capital is able to spend cash to produce a great deal of cash, not simply by utilizing inexpensive natural materials as land, water, minerals and forests, but additionally by making use of speculation along with other non-productive means as well as by exploiting inexpensively skilled as well as unskilled labour. A crucial objective is additionally in order to entice foreign capital and reinforce the role of Indian businesses in the struggle for export markets as well as to get overseas technology and capital. The Economic Policy model pursues the aim of transforming India into a world power by making it an office, a laboratory (for biotech and pharmaceutical companies, for example), along with a factory for international capital, according to (relatively) affordable labour, both unskilled and skilled. In order to do this goal, the important company creates certain needs on the state, including: deregulation of private companies; privatisation of government companies; trade liberalisation; giving of authorization to overseas capital to personal companies in India; enactment of other incentives and tax cuts for businesses; reduction or maybe total withdrawal of government advantages for the poor; and finish freedom to employ as well as fire labour.

The Economic Policy isn't simply about economic issues. This's since it may ensure ideological and political conditions for several accumulation strategies. "Political conditions" in this instance means judicial coercion and express repression (like the suppression of democratic rights; to be discussed later). "Ideological conditions" here refers to the promotion of market fetishism in all of spheres of daily life, including social consciousness. Connected with market fetishism are actually the strategies of getting high rapidly by any means and of the marketplace as the dominant technique of supporting the very poor (hence the acceptance of such items as micro-credit and self-help groups in the discourse of development, pleasantly encouraged by the state as well as civil society groups).

Conclusion

India's development encounter has attracted considerable interest in economic development. A lot of the literature focuses on the failure of India's first procedure of "State directed" improvement with a solid inward-looking bias in the development technique of its. It's been well demonstrated exactly how India's extended technique of import substitution was followed by a paradigm shift towards a far more liberalized open economy model of improvement of the 1990s. India's profitable emergence of the world economy has frequently been linked to this liberalized trade as well as manufacturing policy regime. Basically, the current literature on India's development encounter analyses the economic functionality of it's in an effort to associate it with the wide theoretical contours of outward versus inward-looking industrialization and development.

Neo-liberal economic liberalisation hence discovered changes in policy stance that is economic in each monetary and fiscal policy matters. With the government introducing self-control on fiscal deficit through Fiscal Responsibility and Budget Management Act to consist of fiscal deficit, the fiscal policy alternative of boosting government expenditure, flat when needed, is actually gone. At exactly the same time, this's a stage that witnessed overwhelming concessions or maybe financial assistance provided to the capital at the price of work to draw in private - especially foreign investment.

The state laws as well as controls in sector had been transformed to facilitate the market-led expansion of industries. The monetary policy, on the additional hand, became a lot more focused on inflation targeting. As compared to the earlier period of post-Independent planning as well as state-led transition, this particular stage of transition registered a lot more remarkable economic growth rates which before remained very unthinkable. Gone are actually the days of what's widely known as Hindu Rate of Growth, the phrase coined by Raj Krishna to explain the reasonable growth documents of the planning days. The pose of economic planning even went by transformation with express led funding targeting no longer staying the process of planning.